SPECTROSCOPY IN SUPERCONDUCTORS

SPECTROSCOPY IN SUPERCONDUCTORS

By

Dr. K. Sonamuthu

Reader

Deptt. of Physics

J.N.R. Mahavidyalaya

Port Blair

Andaman & Nicobar

DPH

DISCOVERY PUBLISHING HOUSE PVT. LTD.

NEW DELHI-110 002

Published by:
Tilak Wasan
DISCOVERY PUBLISHING HOUSE PVT. LTD.
4831/24, Prahlad Street, Ansari Road
Darya Ganj, New Delhi-110002 (India)
Phone: +91-11-23279245, 43764432
Fax: +91-11-23253475
E-mail: parul.wasan@gmail.com
discoverypublishinghouse@gmail.com
info@discoverypublishinggroup.com
web: www.discoverypublishinggroup.com

***First Edition:* 2011**
ISBN: 978-81-8356-912-5

Preface

In this book it has been discussed that the two different methods of Lattice Dynamics and Normal Coordinate Analysis of a variety of high temperature superconductor. The aim was to provide, in the absence of detailed experimental phonon information on which to base the dynamical models, a sufficiently general and realistic description of the lattice dynamics of these compound to be of use for the prediction and assignment of experimental optic modes and to give a first idea of various phonon properties, such as phonon dispersion curves, phonon densities of states and lattice specific heat. Due the lack of direct experimental input information about the dynamics of high T_c compounds.

A superconductor is characteristics by zero electrical resistance. The temperature below with the resistance of the material vanishes is called transition temperature $T_{c.}$ The second fundamental property of a superconductor is that its normal resistance may be restored if a magnectic field greater than a critical value B_c is applied to the specimen.

The superconductivity, the complete loss of electrical resistance, is destroyed by the application of magnetic induction, B. The magnitude of B necessary to achieve this is the critical induction, B_c , and is a function of temperature rising from zero at T_c to a value $B_c(0)$ at $T = 0$ K. The magnetic flux is completely expelled from the interior of the superconductor if B is greater than B_c. This is called the Meissner effect. The passage of an electrical current greater than a critical value I_c also destroys superconductivity,

I_c is just that current which results in the critical induction occurring at the surface of the superconductor and is therefore a function of temperature, applied magnetic field and conductor size. Critical inductions, and their practical utility are limited. However, many alloy and compound superconductors have much higher critical inductions, in the range from 1-40 Tesla. The discovery of the high super conducting transition has caused unprecedented world wide activities in the search and characterization of high T_c superconductor is of importance, not only for the overall physical characterization of the role played by the phonons in the superconducting phenomenon.

But also for an assessment of the role played by the phonons in the superconducting phenomenon. Our approach is based on the use of long-range Coulomb potentials and short-range repulsive Born Mayer potentials, as well as ionic polarizabilities, in the framework of the shell model.

The theory of ionic crystals explains the temperature variation of specific heats of many alkali halides reasonable well, but falls to describe the details of vibrational spectra. The three body force shell model (*TSM*) developed from Verma and Singh was reviewed by Cochran on the simple consideration that the electron shell is deformation. This deformation give rise to the three body interactions and accounts for the observed Cauchy discrepancy. The displacement on the other hand introduces the electronic polarization and accounts for the dielectric properties.

The model parameters of *TSM* are usually calculated from the values of elastic constants, the long wave optical vibration frequencies and electronic polarizabiliites of the constituent ions of the solid. The parameters are used to calculate the vibration frequencies, for a number of wave vector along the three high symmetry directions. In the above approaches, the *R, S, T* elements have been set equal to one another. ($R = S = T$).

The study of lattice vibrations and the free carriers is important for the understanding of the physical nature of high temperature superconductors. Raman and far-infrared studies of these superconductors have contributed significantly to the understanding of new class of superconductors. Here an attempt has been made to perform the normal coordinate analysis for the phonon frequencies and the form of the zero wave vector vibrations for the various superconductors.

When the solutions of the secular determinant have been obtained, it is necessary to assign the calculated frequencies to the various modes of motion.

The potential energy distribution rather than the normalized amplitudes is a more satisfactory quantity to use in band assignments; for a vibration of frequency $\tilde{o}_a$, associated with a normal coordinate Q_a.

This book deals with the comparative study between Lattice dynamics and normal coordinate analysis of high temperature superconductors $GdBa_2Cu_3O_7$, $SmBa_2Cu_3O_7$, $EuBa_2Cu_3O_6$, $Tl_2Ca_3Ba_2Cu_4O_{12}$, $Tl_2Ba_2Cu_1O_6$, $TlCa_3Ba_2Cu_4O_{11}$, $Tl_2Ca_2Ba_2Cu_3O_{10}$ and $TlCaBa_2Cu_2O_7$. In the present investigation the lattice dynamical calculations and normal coordinate analysis yield same phonon frequency a bridge between Solid State Physics and Spectroscopy to understand the mechanism of superconductivity. Raman and infrared studies of these HTSC have contributed significantly to their understanding. The assignment of the spectral features to specific lattice vibrations would be an important step in understanding their role in superconductivity.

In this book, two different methods viz, lattice dynamical study and normal coordinate analysis yielded the same phonon frequency for high temperature superconductor $GdBa_2Cu_3O_7$, $SmBa_2Cu_3O_7$, $EuBa_2Cu_3O_6$, $Tl_2Ca_3Ba_2Cu_4O_{12}$, $Tl_2Ba_2Cu_1O_6$, $TlCa_3Ba_2Cu_4O_{11}$, $Tl_2Ca_2Ba_2Cu_3O_{10}$ and $TlCaBa_2Cu_2O_7$. It is also seen from the tables, that the agreement between the calculated and observed frequencies wherever available are very good for the systems under consideration.

Therefore, it is concluded that metal-oxide (Cu-O) plays an important role for the occurrence of superconductivity. The Raman scattering has provided direct evidence for strong electron–phonon interaction in the high T_c superconducting oxides. The vibrational frequencies calculated by the methods of Lattice Dynamics and Normal Coordinate Analysis are compared and they appear to be in good agreement, which is confirmed by the Potential Energy Distribution calculation.

DR. K. SONAMUTHU

JNRM, Port Blair

Contents

CHAPTER

1

Introduction

The discovery of superconductivity at high temperature in a number of oxides[1-3] has caused a revival of interest in oxides in general. Before the discovery of superconductivity in these materials, perhaps their most interesting topic was the insulator metal transitions[4-8] as exhibited by Ti_2O_3, V_2O_3 and VO_2. Interpretation on this transition, however, was complicated by the fact that there was simultaneous changes in the electronic, magnetic and structural properties and it is still difficult to identify which is the cause and which is the effect. More recently Zaanen, Sawatzky, and Allen[9] (ZSA) have develop a general framework for oxides, which has been recently shown[10] to be able to account for differences between metallic and insulating conductivity for a wide variety of oxides.

In addition to introducing a new type of insulator metal transition, this work provides solid experimental data on high temperature superconductor. Such information is fundamental to the assumptions underlying theoretical models for oxides, which should perhaps first concentrate on understanding such basic transition before attempting to explain the relatively suitable mechanism of high temperature superconductivity.

Metallic conductivity was observed[11] $LaNiO_3$, whereas $LuNiO_3$ and $YNiO_3$ appeared[12] insulating based on magnetic susceptibility measurements, suggested antiferro-magnetic ordering at T_N = 130 and 145k, respectively. Very recently insulator metal transition where discover in Sm[13], Nd,[13-14] Pr compound. In which the transition temperature was strongly decreased with increasing size of the earth rare ion. Associated with this insulator metal transition, a small discontinues decrease. Here we report a systematic of insulator metal and magnetic phase transition in the $RNiO_3$ series, including new data for the Gd and Sm compounds as well as for some solid solution between those of Sm, Gd, Pr and La, in order to map out the behaviours of these phase transition, so that we can better understand their inter relationship and physical origins.

In this work it has been discussed the lattice dynamics of of a variety of high temperature superconductor. The aim was to provide, in the absence of detailed experimental phonon information on which to base the dynamical models, a sufficiently general and realistic description of the lattice dynamics of these compound to be of use for the prediction and assignment of experimental optic modes and to give a first idea of various phonon properties, such as phonon dispersion curves, phonon densities of states and lattice specific heat. Due the lack of direct experimental input information about the dynamics of high T_c compounds, we had to base our lattice dynamical approach on what was known about the lattice dynamics of related compound, such as perovskites and metal oxides. It will be clear that or model may have to be extended, when experimental phonon dispersion data of the high T_c compounds themselves becomes generally available. We base our calculation on the interaction potential between pairs of ions. We separate this potential into long range Coulomb part and short range overlap part for which we assume Born-Mayer potentials. In addition to the two body potential, we take into account displacement—induced deformation of the electronic densities in the framework of a shell model because of the use of short-range potential, the eigen values and eigen vector are obtained in the same approximation, assuring that the latter have real physical meaning. This is by no means assured for the eigen vector obtained from force constant models for complicated structure like high T_c compounds.

It is generally believed, that is needed to signpost the way to the development of materials with high critical temperature, even to room temperature and above, is the formulation of a proper theoretical understanding of superconductivity in these materials. Many experimental studies suggest an intimate relationship between phonons, and the superconducting transition in the high T_c oxides. For example, Raman frequencies and line widths, elastic constants and thermal conductivity all show changes around T_c. Nevertheless, there is not a well-developed theory to explain how the phonons are related to T_c. In conventional superconductors, the role of phonons is well established. However, in high T_c superconductors, the role played by phonons is controversial. Even if they do not mediate the pairing mechanism, they are likely to play an important subsidiary role. Hence there is much interest in the phonon structure of these materials.

The normal state and superconducting properties are believed to arise from the strongly correlated motion of the electronic charge carries (electrons or holes) in the CuO_2 planes that essentially define the layered cuprate HTSC. The other cations and oxygen atom in the structure provides structural stability and control the number of charge carries in the CuO_2 planes.

The Raman spectroscopy of HTSC explains that the role played by the phonons in the mechanism of superconductivity in the perovskite family of superconductors is not fully understood although a large series of experimental results has shown considerable coupling of some phonons to electronic excitation in these systems. Optical spectroscopy and especially Raman and Infrared spectroscopy revealed strong direct influences of the changes in the electronic states to the phonon at the center of the Brillouin.

This book is planned for 5 chapters. Chapter 1 gives brief introduction of high temperature superconductor.

Chapter 2 deals with the general instructions of high temperature superconductor, with an emphasis on the two properties of superconductors. One is that the temperature below which the resistance of the material vanishes is called transition temperature T_c. The second fundamental property of a superconductor is that its normal resistance may be restored if a magnetic field greater than a critical value B_c is applied to the specimen. It is zero at T_c and as the temperature is reduced it increases, following the parabolic law $B_c = B_0\{1-[T/T_c]^2\}$. The magnitude of B to achieve this is the critical induction. Further, the basic structural aspects of high T_c cuprates is also explained in this chapter. The cuprate superconductors like La-M-Cu-O, Y-Ba-CuO, Bi-Sr-Ca-Cu-O and Tl-Ba-Ca-Cu-O are widely worked on groups. Holes are the majority current carries in these systems. Finally this chapter ends with the recent developments, applications and future prospects.

Chapter 3 deals with the lattice dynamics of high temperature superconductors. The assignments of spectral features to specify lattice vibrations are an important step to understand their role of superconductivity. Raman and infrared studies have contributed significantly for the explication of high T_c superconductor mechanics. For the basic understanding of the physical properties such as thermal, elastic, dielectric and infrared properties, the knowledge of the actual form of phonon frequency spectrum is required which can be achieved by means of theoretical models of lattice dynamics.

The lattice dynamics of $GdBa_2Cu_3O_7$, $SmBa_2Cu_3O_7$, $EuBa_2Cu_3O_6$, $Tl_2Ca_3Ba_2Cu_4O_{12}$, $Tl_2Ba_2Cu_1O_6$, $TlCa_3Ba_2Cu_4O_{11}$, $Tl_2Ca_2Ba_2Cu_3O_{10}$ and $TlCaBa_2Cu_2O_7$ have been investigated using Three Body Force Shell Model (TSM). A substantial

Concentration of electrons along the bending directions is required to counter balance the self-repulsion of a structure. This distribution of electrons gives rise to the three body forces. In the present work, a Shell model is developed by reformulating the original TSM which takes care of the effect of many body interactions in the lattice potential. In the present work, the lattice dynamical calculation is based on the use of long-range Coulomb potentials and short-range repulsive potentials as well as the ionic polarizabilities, in the framework of the Shell model. Here, the various interactions between the ions are treated in a more general way without making them numerically equal.

In chapter 4, the essential of normal co-ordinate analysis is discussed, which explains the picture of the normal coordinate analysis of the spectral frequencies of the high temperature of $GdBa_2Cu_3O_7$, $SmBa_2Cu_3O_7$, $EuBa_2Cu_3O_6$, $Tl_2Ca_3Ba_2Cu_4O_{12}$, $Tl_2Ba_2Cu_1O_6$, $TlCa_3Ba_2Cu_4O_{11}$, $Tl_2Ca_2Ba_2Cu_3O_{10}$ and $TlCaBa_2Cu_2O_7$ are presented in this chapter.

This chapter further deals with the normal coordinate calculation was performed using the programmes GMAT and FPERT given by Fuhrer *et al.* The evaluated Raman frequencies agree close to the available observed infrared and Raman frequencies giving further support to the present assignment. The results and discussion are given in detail in the respective subsections.

To check whether the chosen set of vibrational frequencies makes maximum contribution to the potential energy associated with the normal coordinate frequencies of the superconducting material, the potential energy distribution was calculated using the equation :

$$PED = (F_{ij}\ L^2{}_{ik})/\ddot{e}k$$

Chapter 5 deals with the comparative study of phonon frequencies obtained from Lattice Dynamics and Normal Coordinate Analysis of high temperature superconductors $GdBa_2Cu_3O_7$, $SmBa_2Cu_3O_7$, $EuBa_2Cu_3O_6$, $Tl_2Ca_3Ba_2Cu_4O_{12}$, $Tl_2Ba_2Cu_1O_6$, $TlCa_3Ba_2Cu_4O_{11}$, $Tl_2Ca_2Ba_2Cu_3O_{10}$ and

$TlCaBa_2Cu_2O_7$. It is interesting to note that the lattice dynamical calculations and normal coordinate analysis yield same phonon frequency a bridge between Solid State Physics and Spectroscopy to understand the mechanism of superconductivity.

REFERENCES

1. A.W. Sleigh, J.I. Gillson, and P.E. Biertedt *Solid State Commun*, 25(1975) **17**.
2. I.G. Bednorz and K.A. Mullre, *Z. Phys*. B64, (1986) **189**.
3. R.J. Cava, B. Batlogg, J.J. Krajewski, R. Farrow, and L. WRupp, nature (London) 332. (1988) **814**.
4. J.B.Goodenough, *Prog. Solid State Chem*. 5, (1971) 149.
5. D. Adler. radiat. Eff, 4, (1970) **123**.
6. N.f., Mott, *Metal-Insulator Transistion* (Taylor and Francis, London (1974).
7. D.B. McWhan, J. P. Remeika, T.M. Rice, W.F. Brinkman, J. Maita, and A. Menth, *Phys. Rev. Lett*. 27, (1971) **941** *Phys, RevB5*,(1972).
8. M. Yethiraj, J. Solid State Chem.88, (1990) **53**, and *reference therem.*
9. Zaanen. G.A, Sawarzky, and J.W. Allen, *Phys. Rev*. Lett. 55, (1985) **418**, J. Zaanen and G.A., Sawarzky, J. Solid State chem., 88. (1990).
10. J.B. Torrance, P, Lacorre, C. Asavaroengchai, and R.M. Metzger, *J.Solid State Chem*. 90, (1991) **168**; *Physica* C 182, (1991) **135**; *J.B. Solid State. Chem*. 96, (1992) **59**.
11. J.B. Goodenough and P.M. Raccah. *J. Appl. Phys*. 36, (1965) **1031**; A.Wold, B. Post and E. banks, J. Amer. *Chem. Soc*. 79, (1957) **4911**.
12. G.Demazeau, A. marbeuf, M. Pouchard, and P. Hagenmuller, *J. Solid State Chem* 3, (1971) **582**.
13. P. Lacorre, J.B. Torrance, J. Pannetier, A.I. Nazzal, P.W. Whan, and T.C. Haung, *J. Solid State. Chem*. 91, (1991) **225**.
14. K. Vassiliou, M. Hornbostel, R. Ziebarth, and F.J. DiSalvo, and *Solid State. Chem*. 81, (1989) **208**

CHAPTER

2

Review Literature

Origin of High Temperature Superconductors

A superconductor shows vanishing resistance below a characteristic temperature called the transition temperature T_c. Soon after Onnes discovery in 1991, other researchers found that lead become superconducting below 7.2 K and tin below 3.7 K. Until 1986, the higher superconducting transition temperature was 23.21 K in Nb_3Ge as found by Cavater. The new era of high temperature superconductors began in 1986, with the announcement of T_c about 30 K by Nobel prize winners, George Bednorz and Alexander Muller in Lanthanum-Barium-copper oxide[1] [La-Ba-Cu-O systems]. But the actual break through occurred only after 76 years of the discovery of the phenomenon of superconductivity and has prompted unprecedented interest and excitement. This was by the discovery of superconductivity in an oxide with a T_c above the boiling point of liquid nitrogen by Paul Chu and his co-workers in 1987. Later, Chu et al[2] showed that the T_c of La-Sr-Cu-O could be raised from 35 K to 50 K by applying pressure. Then as an attempt to mimic the effect of increased pressure by chemical substitution, a rare earth ion, namely Yttrium was used, which is smaller than Lanthanum and thus a higher T_c was obtained owing to the included internal pressure. This resulted in the discovery of a new compound, subsequently confirmed as $YBa_2Cu_3O_7$ with a T_c of 90 K[3]. The intense research effort thus unleashed has led to the discovery of further compounds: Bi-Sr-Ca-Cu-O with T_c up to 120 K[4] and Tl-Ba-Ca-Cu-O with T_c as high as 130 K[5], including the remarkable C_{60} based fullerene compounds[6] in which T_c in Rb-Tl-C has been claimed at 42.5 K. Then C_{60} based superconductors provide another totally new arena for studies of novel superconducting organic materials with great future promise for even higher T_c's. In March 1993, the mercury based layered copper oxides $HgBa_2CuO_{4+x}$ (Hg-1201)[7] came to light, the latest of the brood has set a record of 133 K for the superconducting transition temperature. Recently, Chu *et al.*[8] have shown that the mercury based systems have a T_c of 160 K and this is believed to be the highest critical temperature achieved so far. Although the majority of high temperature superconductors (HTSC) are *p*-type, involving hole doping of the planes, a number of *n*-type electron doped HTSC such as $Nd_{2-x}Ce_xCuO_4$[9] have also been discovered.

Basic Characteristic of Superconductors

A superconductor is characteristics by zero electrical resistance[10]. The temperature below with the resistance of the material vanishes is called transition temperature T_c.

The second fundamental property of a superconductor is that its normal resistance may be restored if a magnectic field greater than a critical value B_c is applied to the specimen. It is zero at T_c and as the temperature is reduced it increases, following the parabolic law

$$B_c = B_0\{1-[T/T_c]^2\}$$

It tends to a constant value B_0 as T approaches 0 K.

Superconductors allow the flow of electric current under zero voltage. Beyond a certain critical current, the material develops, the voltage drop and original conduction is recorded. J_c is the largest current density the material can carry under zero voltage in the superconducting state. Associated with an electric current, there will be a magnetic field. Hence, if a superconductor carries a current such that the field that produced is equal to B_c, the resistance of the sample is restored. So superconducting state is characterized by $J < J_c$[11].

A superconductor exhibits perfect diamagnetism with $B = 0$ inside it. This phenomenon is called the meissener effect whereby a superconductor expels magnectic flux from within and becomes a perfect diamagnet provided the external applied field is small. The conditions defining superconducting state are

$E = 0$ (from the absence of resistivity)

$B = 0$ (from Meissner effect)

Depending upon the magnetic behaviour, superconductors are classified as Type I and Type II[12] (*See Fig. 2.1 on next page*). The materials that always expel the flux completely before returning to the normal state are classified as Type I superconductors or pure superconductors. Here B_c, the strength of the applied magnetic field of the applied magnetic field is parabolic. B_0 is the extrapolated value of B_c at $T = 0$. Except for Vanadium and Niobium all elements are Type I superconductors.

The Type II superconductors remain superconducting upto a very high magnetic field even with the penetration of the magnetic flux. There are two critical fields in the Type II superconductors: The lower critical field B_{c1} and the upper critical field B_{c2}. The flux is completely expelled only upto the field B_{c1}. So, in applied fields smaller than B_{c1}, Type II superconductors behave just like Type I superconductors. Above B_{c1}, the flux partially penetrates into the material until upper critical field B_{c2} is reached. Above B_{c2} the material returns to its normal state. The superconductor is in a mixed or vortex state between B_{c1} and B_{c2}. The Meissner effect is only partial. For all applied fields $B_{c1} < B < B_{c2}$, magnetic flux partially penetrates the superconducting specimen in the microscopic filaments called vortices.

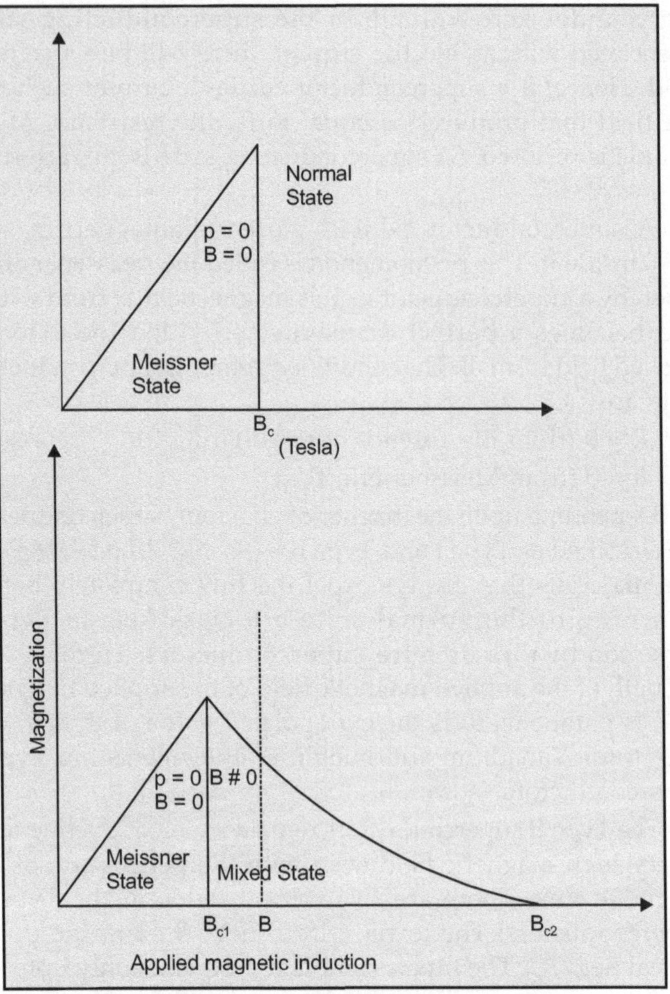

Fig. 2.1 : Type I and Type II superconductors

Phenomenon of Superconductivity

Superconductivity, the complete loss of electrical resistance, is destroyed by the application of magnetic induction, *B*. The magnitude of *B* necessary to achieve this is the critical induction, B_c, and is a function of temperature rising from zero at T_c to a value $B_c(0)$ at $T = 0$ K. In the so-called Type I superconductors, the magnetic flux is completely expelled from the interior of the superconductor if B is greater than B_c. This is called the Meissner effect. The passage of an electrical current greater than a critical value I_c also destroys superconductivity, I_c is just that current which results in the critical induction occurring at the surface of the superconductor and is therefore a function of temperature, applied magnetic field and conductor size. Critical inductions, and their practical utility are limited. However, many alloy and compound superconductors have much higher critical inductions, in the range from 1-40 Tesla. These materials are termed as Type II superconductors and they have an incomplete Meissner effect. Magnetic flux enters the body of the superconductor in the form of localized flux lines, ach carrying a single quantum of magnetic flux, Φ_0. when a current, of density J flows in a Type II superconductors in a magnetic induction B, the flux line experiences a Lorentz force $F_L = J \times B$. The critical Lorentz force is equal to the total pinning force per unit volume F_p, which is a function of both temperature and magnetic induction.

The critical current density is the most important parameter of the superconductor for the majority of applications. In the case of a normal conductor, resistance arises because electron lose momentum which they have acquired from the electric field, by scattering collisions with defects of the crystalline lattice. In the superconducting state, these collision still occur but pairs of electrons act in a co-operative manner to ensure that there is no net change in momentum. In conventional superconductors, the motion of the two electrons in a pair is described by the Bardeen, Cooper and Schrieffer (BCS) theory of superconductivity.

BCS Theory of Superconductivity

The microscopic theory put forward by Bardeen,Cooperand Schriefer (BCS), in 1957, provides the better quantum explanation of superconductivity and accounts very well for all the properties exhibited by the superconductors. This theory involves the electron interactions through phonons as mediators. The basis of the formulation of BCS theory are the two experimental conclusion namely the isotope effect and the variation of specific heat of superconductor. This all suggest that non-zero transition temperature is a consequence of the finite mass of the ions which can contribute phonons by their vibrations. One can interpret the interaction between the lattice and electron as the constant emission and re-absorption (creation and annihilation) of phonons. BCS showed that the basic interaction responsible for superconductivity appear to be that of a pair of electrons by means of an interchange of virtual phonons. The lowering of electron energy implies that the force between the two electrons is attractive. This type of interaction is strongest when the two electrons have equal and opposite momenta and spins. This interaction can also be interpreted as the electron-electron interaction through phonons as the mediator. If the phonon energy exceeds electronic energy, the interaction is attractive.

The fundamental postulate of BCS theory is that superconductivity when occurs an attractive interaction between two electrons, by means of phonon exchange, dominates the usual repulsive Coulomb interaction. An attractive interaction between electrons can lead to a ground state separated from excited state by an energy gap. The energy difference between the free state of the electron and the paired state appears as the energy gap at the Fermi surface. The normal electrons states are above the energy gap and the superconducting electrons states are below the energy gap at the Fermi surface. Energy gap is a function of temperature, and it is maximum at absolute zero. At $T = T_c$, pairing is dissolved and energy gap reduces to zero. Across the energy gap there are many excited states for the superconducting Cooper pairs. The critical field, the thermal properties and most of the electromagnetic properties are consequences of the energy gap.

Superconductivity occurs when such an attractive interaction between two electrons, by means of a phonon

$x = 0.15$ and $x = 0.2$ for Ba and Sr. The La ion in $La_{2-x}M_xCuO_4$ can be replaced by Pr, Nd, Gd and other rare earth ions without losing superconductivity.

YBCO (123) System

The $YBa_2Cu_3O_{7-\delta}$ (*Fig. 2.3*) has an orthorhombic structure with two Cu-O sheets in the a-b plane and Cu-O chains along the b-axis[14]. The unit cell dimensions have been determined by electron and x-ray diffractions have identified the structure as being related to a cubic perovskite with one of the cubic axis a triplet. The oxygen content δ determines the lattice parameter. When $\delta \sim 0.6$, the structure becomes tetragonal. In $YBa_2Cu_3O_{7-\delta}$ also varies with δ and the material becomes

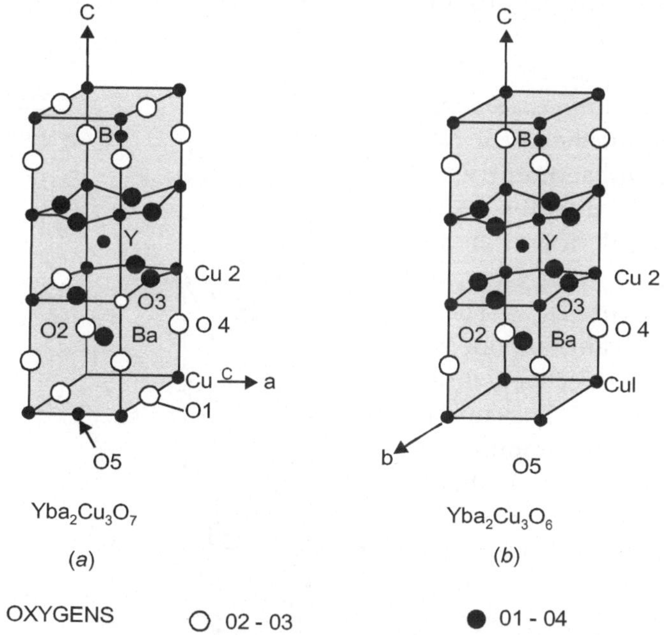

Fig. 2.3 : Structures of $YBa_2Cu_3O_{7-8}$
(*a*) Orthorhombic structure of superconducting δ = 0 Phase
(*b*) Tetragonal structure of non-superconducting δ = 1 with no Cu-O chains

non-superconducting at $\delta = 0.6$. T_c remains around 90K upto $\delta = 0.2$ and then shows a plateau at 60K when $\delta = 0.3 - 0.4$, T_c is 45K when $\delta = 0.5$. Structural studies show that oxygen may be ordered when $\delta = 0.5$ and 0.75. In $\delta = 0.5$ composition fully oxygenated CuO chain are present along the b-axis, alternately with fully vacant O(1) site. No clear are oxygen ordering has been found in $\delta = 0.3 - 0.4$. There is a tendency for the oxygen atoms vacancies to occupy a single chain and the $YBa_2Cu_3O_{7-\delta}$ compounds with $0 < \delta < 1$ tend to have ordered arrays of completely oxygen depleted chain. When $\delta = 1$ there is no chains.

Bi Sr Ca Cu O Systems

From early reports that $Bi_2Sr_2CaCuO_6$ is a superconductor with a maximum T_c~22K depending on the Bi/Sr ratio and subsequently bismuth cuprates of the general formula $Bi_2(CaSr)_{n+1}Cu_nO_{2n+4}$ are discovered[15-17]. The Tc value ranges from 90 – 100K respectively for n = 2 and n = 3. The cuprates are orthor-hombic and contain Cu-O sheets, besides two Ca, Sr-O layers and two Bi-O layers (*Fig. 2.4*). In this system Tc increases with the number of CuO_2 layers. However, the usual problem encountered with then bismuth cuprates is the lack of

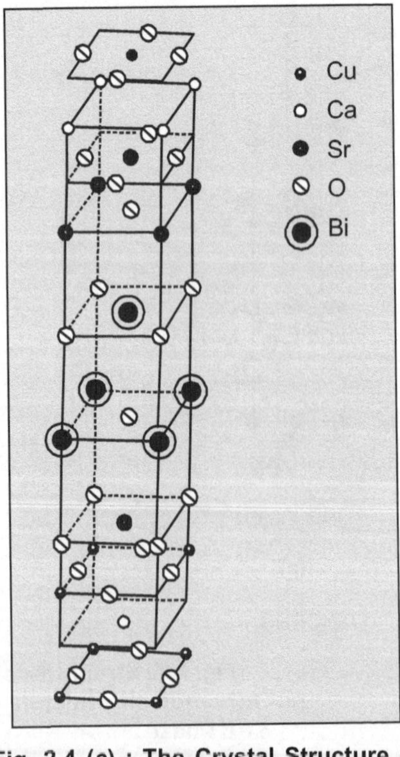

Fig. 2.4 (*a*) : The Crystal Structure of $Bi_2CaSr_2Cu_2O_8$

phase purity.The divalent Ca ion in the bismuth cuprates can be replaced by trivalent rare-earth ion as in $Bi_2Ca_{1-x}Ln_xSr_2Cu_2O_{8+\delta}$ (Ln = Y or rare-earth.)

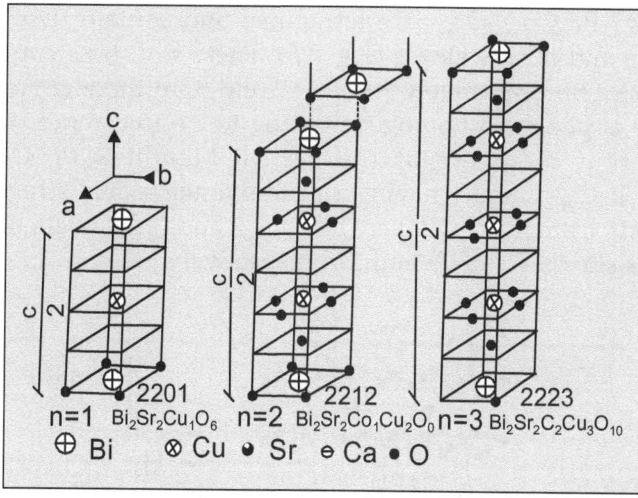

Fig. 2.4 (*b*) : Structure of the family of Bi-based ceramic Superconductors

Tl Ba Ca Cu O Systems

In the thallium system, there are two series of compounds, $Tl_1Ba_2Ca_{n-1}Cu_nO_{2n+3}$ and $Tl_2Ba_2Ca_{n-1}Cu_nO_{2n+4}$ (n=1 to5), which can be modelled as an interleaving of rock salt and defective perovskite layers[18-19]. For example, $TlBa_2CuO_5$ can be thought of as a layer of copper oxide sandwiched between two layers of barium oxide, which is in turn sandwiched between two layers of thallium oxide. This compound, 1201, is not superconducting. A second copper layer can be inserted into the sandwich provided; it is separated from the first by a calcium layer. This gives the 1212 compound, which has a T_c of approximately 90K. A second calcium layer allows the insertion of a third copper layer giving the 1223 compound with T_c increased to 116K. The corresponding series of compounds with T_c increased to 116K.The corresponding series of compounds with the double thallium layers are somewhat higher values of $T_{c,}$ for 2223, the highest T_c is at 128K. Thallium cuprates of the general formula $Tl_2Ca_{n-1}Ba_2Cu_{+9n}O_{2n+4}$ are tetragonal and contain two Tl-O layers and nCu-O sheets (*Fig. 2.5*). The T_cs of these cuprates are 80, 110, respectively for *n*+1, 2 and 3. In these cuprates , there is phasic in homogeneity due to co-occurrence of the different members of the series. Members of $TlCa_{n-1}Ba_2Cu_nO_{2n+3}$ family having a primitive tetragonal structure, contain a single Tl-O layer. The *n* + 2 and 3 members of the series shows T_cs of 90 and 115 respectively.

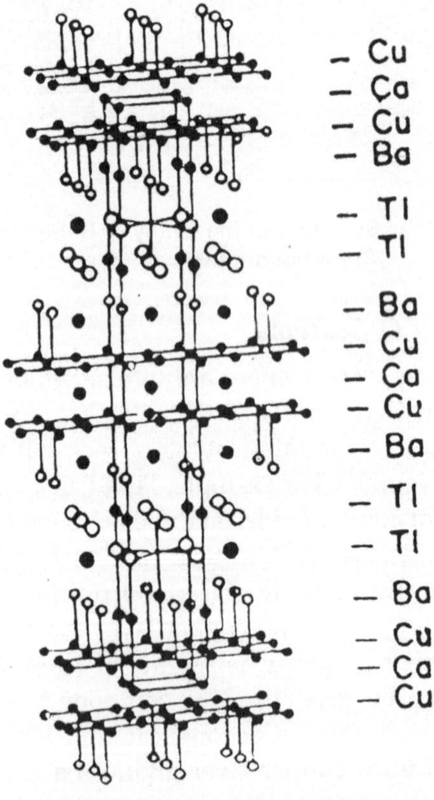

Fig. 2.5 : The Crystal Structure of $Tl_2CaBa_2Cu_2O_{8+\delta}$

Thallium cuprates with $n>3$ have been characterized but T_c does not increase beyond $n = 3$. Partial substitution of Tl by Pb or Ca by a rare earth as in $Tl_{0.5}Pb_{0.5}CaSr_2Cu_2O_{6+\delta}$ (T~90K) and $TlCa_{0.5}Sr_2Cu_2O_{6-\delta}$ (T~90K) give rise to super-conductivity. Pb in this Thallium cuprateis in the 4+ state, making $Tl_{0.5}Pb_{0.5}CaSr_2Cu_2O_{6-\delta}$ and $TlCa_{0.5}Ln_{+0.5}Sr_2Cu_2O_{6+\delta}$ isoelectronic.

It may be noted that in the Bi and Tl cuprates as well as in the 1-2-3 compounds, there is always ca or / and Ba. At the same time superconducting Tl cuprates of the formula $TlSr_{n+1-x}Ln_xCu_nO_{2n+3}$ have been prepared as also cuprates of the type $Tl_{1-x}Pb_xSr_{n+1}Cu_nO_{2n+3}$, which do not contain Ca or Ba or even a rare earth.

Towards Applications

Inspite of numerous difficulties, the improvement in the superconducting properties has opened the door to a host of futuristic applications. The basic properties of the superconductors electrical have been successfully exploited for their practical applications. The three fundamental parameters that determine the economic feasibility for the applications are : (*i*) critical temperature (T_c), (*ii*) critical current (J_c) and (*iii*) critical magnectic field (H_{c2}). The higher the above three values, the better will be the practical applications. The discovery of HTSC has unique challenges for the electric power industry. It holds the promise of a new technology, which becomes economically viable only in the area of large-scale power generation and distribution. The large-scale application of superconductors in power industry depends on two basic properties :

(*i*) Its ability to carry very high current with no or very little loss

(*ii*) Its ability to produce medium to high magnetic field

The first property is used in power transmission while the second in power generation and storage.

Power Transmission

Since superconductors exhibit zero resistance below T_c, there is no energy dissipation (I^2R loss) associated with the flow of current through it. Hence, superconductors have been proposed for power transmission cables for loss-less transmission. Many superconductors can carry, without energy loss, 100 to 1000 times larger current densities compared to normal conductors like copper. The need for cryogenic apparatus for cooling effectively excludes them for small-scale transmission due to high costs. It becomes economically now exists for power transmission and in electronic circuitry employing liquid nitrogen as the coolant.

Power Storage

Another area, where large-scale application of superconductors are conceptualized is in the area of superconducting magnetic energy storage. Here one utilizes the properties of a superconductor to sustain very high magnetic field. With d.c. operating the current in a superconducting coil short-circuited at its ends, flows indefinitely so that superconductor coils can be used as an inductive storage device. The most attractive application of such a device will be in load balancing in existing power grids.

Superconducting Magnets

The most important application of superconductors is in magnets. The success of superconductivity started with small laboratory magnets and extended through NMR to whole body magnetic resonance medical imaging (MRI). Superconducting magnets are also used in nuclear physics for the acceleration and focussing of particle beams and in particle detecting bubble chambers.

REFERENCES

1. J.G. Bednorz and K.A. Muller, *Z. Phys.* **B 64**,189,1986.
2. C.W. Chu, P.H. Hor, R.L. Mrg and L.Gao, Z.J. Huang and Y.Q. Wang, *Phy.Rev. Lett.* **58** , 405, 1987.
3. M.K.Wu, J.R. Ashburn, C.J. Torng, P.H.Hor, R.L. Meng, L.Gao, Z.J.Huag, Y.Q. Wang and C.W. Chu, *Phy.Rev.Lett.* **58**, 908, 1987.

4. H.Maeda, Y. Tanaka, M.Fukutomi and T.Asano, *Jpn. J.Appli.Phys.* **27,** L209, 1988.
5. Z.Z.Sheng, A.M.Hermann, A.E.Ali, C.Almasan, J.Estrada, D.Datta and R.J.Matson, *Phys.Rev.Lett.* **60** 937, 1988.
6. M.J.Rosseinksy, A.P. Ramirez, S.H. Glarum, R.C. Haddon, A.F. Hebard, T.T.M. Palstra, A.R.Kortan, S.M.Zahurak, A.V.Makhija, *Phys.Rev.Lett.* **66** 2830, 1991.
7. S.N.Putlin, E.Vantipov, O.Chmaissen and M.Marezio, *Nature,* **362,** 226,1993.
8. C.W. Cu, New *Scientist,* 1993.
9. Y. Tokura, H.Takagi and S.Uchida, *Nature ,* **337** 334, 1989.
10. C. Kittle, *'Introduction to Solid State Physics',* John Wiley & Sons 1976.
11. S.V.Subramanyam and E.S.Rajagopal, *'High Temperature Super-conductors',* Wiley Eastern Ltd. 1989.
12. A.C. Rose-Innes and E.H.Phoderick, *'Introduction to Super-conductivity',* Pergamon Press Ltd., 1978.
13. P. Ganguly and C.N.R. Rao, *J.Solidstate Chem.***58,***193,1984*
14. A.P. Litvinchuk, C.Thomson and C. Cardona *Solidstate communications* Vol. **83**, 1992, 343-347.
15. C.Michael, MHerview, M.M.Borel, A.Gradin, F.Deslanders, J. Provost and B. Raveau, *Z Phys.* **B68**, 421, 1987.
16. A Khurana, *Phys. Today* **41** (No. 4), 21, 1988.
17. H. Maeda, Y. Tanaka, M. Fukutomi and T. Asano, *Jap. J.Appl. Phys* **27,** L209, 1988
18. A.D. Kulkarni and W. de wette, J. Prade and U. Schroder W.Kress, *Physica Review* B 5451, 5457, 1990.
19. M. Krantz, H.J.Rosen, R.M.Macfarlane and V.Y. Lee *Phys.Rev. Vol.* **38** 11962, 11965, 1988.

CHAPTER

3

Lattice Dynamics
Three Body Force Shell Model of $GdBa_2Cu_3O_7$ and $SmBa_2Cu_3O_7$

Introduction

The discovery of the high super conducting transition of the La-Ba-Cu-O system by Bednorz and Muller has caused unprecedented world-wide activities in the search and characterization of high T_c superconductor is of importance, not only for the overall physical characterization of the role played by the phonons in the superconducting phenomenon.

Born-Killermann theory of ionic crystals explains the temperature variation of specific heats of many alkali halides reasonable well, but falls to describe the details of vibrational spectra. The three body force shell model (TSM) developed from Verma and Singh[1] was reviewed by Cochran on the simple consideration that the electron shell is deformation. This deformation give rise to the three body interactions and accounts for the observed Cauchy discrepancy. The displacement on the other hand introduces the electronic polarization and accounts for the dielectric properties. Veram and Agarwal[2] redefined the shell and core charges suitably and hence the basic equation of the model have been modified.

Woods et al.[3] has shown that TSM is equivalent to the breathing shell model (BSM).

Shell Model—Wood's Theory

The connection between the polarization of ions and the repulsive force between them has been considered by Dick and Overhauser[4] and by Hanion and Lawson[5]. They have suggested a 'Shell Model' which is suitable for an ion having a closed electronic configuration given in Fig.3.1. This model has been used with certain extension by Woods et al., to improve the theory of lattice dynamics of ionic crystals.

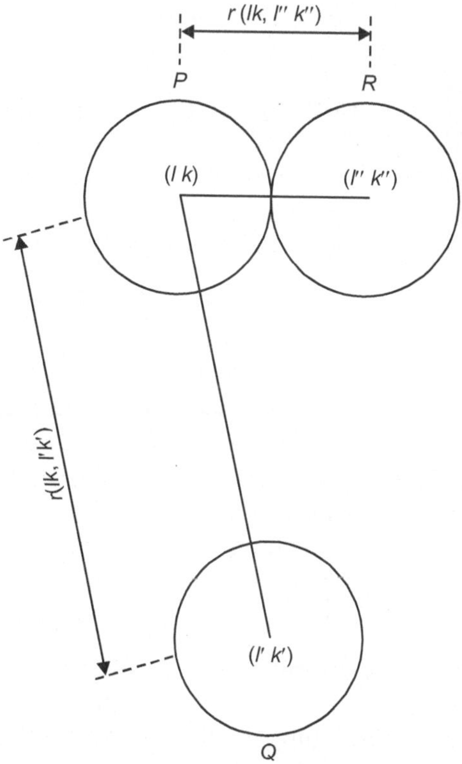

Fig. 3.1 : Schematic representation of TSM

The short range force constants signifying the interaction between shell (S), between cores (D) and between core and shell of the opposite ions (F) and model has been used with certain extension by Wood's et al.[3], to improve the theory of lattice dynamics of ionic crystals. According to Woods, the interaction between two ions is taken to be completely symmetrical. Use of the shell model with both ions polarisable raises the order of the M matrix to twelve, but when the symmetry directions are considered [like (100), (110), (111), etc.],

The short range force constant are further combined to give physically meaningful co-efficients R, A and T which are as follows :

$$R = D + S + 2F \text{ and}$$

$$T = S + F$$

R, T and S are matrices specifying short range interactions. The Mass (M), ionic charge on shell (Y) are column matrices. With these parameters, the equations of motions in the matrix form are given by,

$$-M\,\omega^2 U = (ZC'Z + R)U + (ZC'Y + T)\,W$$

$$0 = (YC'Z + T)U + (YC'Y + S)\,W$$

where M , Z and Y are diagonal matrices representing the mass, ionic charges on the shell. ω is the lattice vibration frequency. R, T and S are matrices specifying the short range interactions between rigid atoms, core-shell and shell - shell respectively. U and W are vectors, U is the amplitude of the displacements of the ions, while YW is the electronic dipole moment on the ions. C' is long range interaction matrix given by,

$$C' = CZ^2\,[\,1 + (12/Z)\,f(a)]_0 + V$$

where C being a matrix describing the electrostatic long range interactions between unit charges as defined by Kellermann[6], V being a matrix describing the three body overlap interaction (long range) as defined by Verma and Singh, $f(a)$ being a function dependent on the overlap integrals of the electron wave functions by Lundquist[7] and the subscript *'o'* implies the evaluation of the quantity in the equilibrium configuration of the lattice. The number of independent parameters in the theory is most easily discussed by considering a wave propagating in a symmetry direction.

The short range interaction for the T matrix are more complicated than for the R matrix. They correspond to two types of interactions; they are the negative ion interaction with the electric dipole moment on the positive ion and the positive ion interaction with the electric dipole moment on the negative ion. These two interactions will not be necessarily be identical. In analogy with the parameters for the short range interaction specifying the R matrix, for nearest neighbour two parameters are defined for each of the two types of interaction.

Three Body Force Shell Model

Verma and Singh developed a TSM based on Lundquist expression for the lattice potential. The potential is given by,

$$\Phi^{TSM} = \phi_m^R$$

$$+ \sum_{lk}\sum_{l'k'}\sum_{l''k''} e\{f_k(r(lk, l'k'))\} Zk'e/r(lk, l'k')$$

The modified overlap repulsive potential is given by

$$\phi_m^R(r) = \Phi^R(r) - ef_k(r(l\,k, l''\,k'')) Z_{k2}\, e/r(lk, l'k')$$

where (R) is the valence of the k type ion and $|(k)| = \varepsilon$. The first term above represent the coulomb energy. The second term is the overlap repulsive energy, coupling the nearest neighbours and the third term is the three-body potential term. The model uses a function $f(a)$ of the nearest neighbour-separation *'a'* connected with the overlap integrals of the electron wave functions and its space derivative df/da as parameters. In addition to the usual parameters of the simple shell model[3], Verma and Singh have derived the coupling co-efficients contributed by three body forces using the above expression. They have studies the long wave length behaviour of NaCl structure. These coupling co-efficients can be used in any theoretical model of ionic crystals. The dynamical matrix which is used in the form where the coupling co-efficients kk^1 are given as

$$\begin{pmatrix} k & k' \\ \alpha & \beta' \end{pmatrix} = -(M_k\, M_k{}') - \frac{1}{2}\begin{pmatrix} k & k' \\ \alpha & \beta' \end{pmatrix}$$

The three-body potential coupling constants have been evaluated for all directions. One can show that, on classical considerations, TSM taken care of the charge transfer between neighbouring ions. In addition to the dipole induced on the sites whereas the simple model accounts only for induced dipole.

The original formulation of TSM suffered from discrepancy in respect of definition of shell and core charges and electronic polarizabilities of ions. This discrepancy was later removed by Verma and Agarwal[2]. An application of the corrected theory the shell and core charges are defined as :

$$X_k\sqrt{Z \times [Z + 12f(a)]} \quad \text{and} \quad Y_k\sqrt{Z \times [Z + 12f(a)]}$$

$$\text{and} \quad X_k + Y_k = \pm 1$$

So that the ion charges comes out to be Z [Z + 12 f' (a)]. Thus in this modified theory, the expressions for electronic (α) and distortion (d) polarizabilities becomes

$$\alpha_1 = \frac{e^2 Y_1^2 Z[Z + 12f(a)]}{k_1 + (T_{11})_o}$$

$$\alpha_2 = \frac{e^2 Y_2^2 Z[Z + 12f(a)]}{k_2 + (T_{22})_o}$$

$$d_1 = \frac{-Y_1 (T_{11})_o \sqrt{Z[Z + 12f(a)]}}{k_1 = (T_{11})_o}$$

$$d_2 = \frac{-Y_2 (T_{22})_o \sqrt{Z[Z + 12f(a)]}}{k_2 = (T_{22})_o}$$

Various ionic crystal have been studied applying the above model. The TSM equation of motion in the matrix form are given by

$$-M\,\omega^2 U = (R + ZC'\,Z)\,U + T\,(T + ZC'\,Y)\,W$$

$$0 = (YC'Z + T')\,U + (YC'Y + S)\,W$$

where
$$Z = X + Y$$

$$ZC' = Z\,[Z + 12\,f(a)]\,C + V$$

where V being the three body potential.

The model parameters of TSM are usually calculated from the values of elastic constants, the long wave optical vibration frequencies and electronic polarizabiliites of the constituent ions of the solid. The parameters are used to calculate the vibration frequencies, for a number of wave vector along the three high symmetry directions. In the above approaches, the R, S, T elements have been set equal to one another. ($R = S = T$).

Modified Theory of Three Body Force Shell Model

The ions in an ionic lattice structure with two atoms per unit cell is denoted by usual symbol (l, k), where the cell index 'l' is the integer triplet (l_1, l_2, l_3) and the basis index $K = 1, 2$. Considering transnational symmetry, the charge-density function around an ion and its charge in equilibrium configuration can be expressed as a series in spherical harmonics.

$$\rho_{1k}^{(r)} = \rho_{1k}^{(r)} - \rho_{1k}^{o(r)}$$

$$= f(r)_o + \sum_{1m}^{-} f(r)Y_{1m} + \sum_{2m} f(r)Y_{1m}$$

Assuming the charge on the ions remain unaltered during vibration, one gets

$$\int_o^\infty 4\pi r_o^2 f(r)dr = 0$$

The above equation is identically satisfied by the simple function.

$$f_o(r) = (1 + a_{1k})^3 g(r) + a_{lk}(r) - g(r)$$

Choosing $g(r) = \rho_k^o(r)$, where $g(r)$ is an arbitrary function and a is a parameter, one obtains

$$4\pi_{1k} r^2 dr\ \rho(r) = 4\pi r_k^2 dr^1 \rho^o(v')$$

Where

$$v' = v + a_{1k}(r)$$

The above equation represents the breathing motion implied in the breathing motion implied in the breathing shell model (BSM). The equation is satisfied only when the upper limit of the integration is infinity. If it is not so, the charge for k-type ion is give by,

$$\int_o^r k[\rho_k^o(r) + f_o(r)]\, 4\pi r^2 dr,$$

Where the positive and negative ionic spaces are finite (r_k)

Even in static condition, the proximity of ions will cause deformation of the charge clouds as suggested by Lundquist[7] is implied in TSM. Defining the original charge of the ion is the absence of the deformation for $f_o(r)$ to be Z_k, one gets

$$\int_o^r k[\rho_k^o(r) + 4\pi r^2 dr_k = Z$$

Hence, the charge on a k-type ion can be deducted from the above equations as

$$\int_o^r k\left(l + a_{1k}^a\right) \rho_k^o[r + a_{1k}(r)] 4\pi r^2 dr \approx Z_k + a_{1k}(r) + Z_k$$

Where $$a_{1k} = 4\pi r^3 f_k^o(r) \frac{a_{1k}}{Z_k}$$

On account of charge mobility and

$$\Sigma(Z_k + a_{1k} Z_k) = 0$$

Hence, $Z_1 = -Z_2$ and $a\,l_1 = a\,l_2$

In effect each ion can have a charge transferred to it from all its neighbours so that a_{1k} is the sum of charge transfers. The energy per unit cell of this modified charge system will be

$$\rho = \frac{-\alpha_{mc^2} Z[Z+12f(r)]}{r} + V_r(12)$$

Where $V_{(r)}$ is overlap repulsive potential. The consideration of the three body interaction within the framework of the shell model can be therefore be done in a simple way including the three body in Columbian interaction terms. The modified TSM by Verma and Singh gives the coulomb matrix as,

$$C^2 = Z\,[Z + 12\,f(a)]\,C + V$$

Where V is the matrix corresponding to the terms containing the first derivative of the charge transfer function $f(r)$. The error in the Verma-Singh model is that the coulomb matrix has been modified while expression for polarizability defining the shell charge has not been suitably modified. Using the suggested core and shell charges along with the coulomb matrix the polarizability equation is,

$$\alpha_k = l_{1k}^2 ybz[Z+12f(a)]/K_\infty + S_o$$

and the distortion polarizability can be defined as

$$d_k = ey_k[Z(Z+12f(a)]^{1/2}/(K_k + S_o)$$

With these corrections, the ionic interactions are treated in a more general was ($R \neq S \neq T$) in the present work. R, S, T are matrices specifying short range core-core, shell-shell and core-shell interactions respectively. $f(a)$ is a function related to the overlapping integrals of elective wave function and V is the matrix of force constants as expressed by Lundquist[7]. The remaining terms have the usual meaning (Cowely *et al.*)[8].

In this approach, the R and C elements are calculated from the dimension less coefficients of Kellermann. The basic and necessary factors for the calculation of model parameters are the same as given in[9,10].

$$C_{11} = \frac{e^2}{4a_o}[-5.112Z[Z+12f(a)]+A+9.3004Z\,(a\,df/da)]$$

$$C_{12} = \frac{e^2}{4a_o^4}[1.391Z\,[Z+12f(a)]+9.3204\,Z\,(a\,df/da)]$$

$$C_{44} = \frac{e^2}{4a_o^4}\{1.391Z\,[Z+12f(a)]\}$$

$$\mu^2_{WL} = R_o{}'\frac{e^2}{V_{fL}}\left(\frac{(Z')^2}{Z^2}\right)\frac{8\pi}{3}(Z\,[Z+12\,f(a)]+6Z\,(a\,df/da))$$

$$\mu^2_{WL} = R_o'\frac{e^2}{VfT}\left(\frac{(Z')^2}{Z^2}\right)\frac{4\pi}{3}(Z\,[Z+12\,f(a)])$$

$$fL = 1+\frac{8\pi\alpha}{3v}Z\,[Z+12f(a)]+6\,Z\,(a\,df/da)/Z^2$$

$$fL = 1-\frac{4\pi\alpha}{3v}Z\,[Z+12\,f(a)]/\,Z^2$$

$$V = 2a_o^3$$

$$Z = Z-d_2+d_1$$

$$R_o = \frac{e^2}{V}(A+2B)$$

$$R_o' = R_o-e^2\frac{d_1^2}{\alpha_1}+\frac{d_2^2}{\alpha_2}$$

Lattice Dynamics of Superconductor

The new high T_c materials contain numerous particles in the unit cell. Thus, in a classical approach to lattice dynamics, a large number of unknown force constants has to be specified. Much attention has been paid, from several points of view, to copper-oxide-based high T_c Superconductors with the formula $GdBa_2Cu_3O_7$ discovered by Cava et al.[12].

However, the rather limited experimental data available for most of the high T_c materials, do not even allow a complete determination of the force constants for the most important interactions. Moreover, a mere fit of force constants to measured frequencies does not necessarily lead to the proper dynamical matrix, since the eigen values alone do not completely specify the eigen value problem. For systems with many particles per unit cell, the eigen vectors obtained by a such procedure may not have a proper physical meaning. Hence, a new procedure is adopted using the Shell Model, for the calculation of lattice vibrations of $GdBa_2Cu_3O_7$ & $SmBa_2Cu_3O_7$ in the framework of a Shell model, based on interatomic short and long range potentials.

The use of short range potentials, as opposed to force constants has important advantages, especially in the case of the high T_c Superconductors: Ordinarily, force constants are determined by least-square fits to measured phonon dispersion curves. In case of high-T_c Superconductors, only a limited number of infrared and Raman frequencies are available for fitting, while due to the large number of particles in the unit cell, a large number of force constants need to be determined. The eigenvectors that are calculated with such a poorly defined force constant model can be quite arbitrary because an eigenvalue problem is incompletely defined by the eigenvalues along. However, the Raman and infrared spectroscopies have been employed to study the interaction of the lattice with the superconducting electronic system.

Theoretical Considerations

Lattice Dynamics of $GdBa_2Cu_3O_7$ based on Shell Model

The study of the lattice dynamics of the high T_c Superconductors is of importance, not only for the overall physical characterization of these compounds, but also for an assessment of the role played by the phonons in the superconducting phenomenon. Our approach is based on the use of long-range Coulomb potentials and short-range repulsive Born Mayer potentials, as well as ionic polarizabilities, in the framework of the shell model.

The calculation of lattice dynamical vibration frequencies of $GdBa_2Cu_3O_7$ system is performed by thee-body force shell model (TSM) calculations. In the shell model calculation the equations of the motion for the code coordinate U and the shell coordinate W are expressed as[13] follows :

$$-M\omega^2 U = (R + ZC'Z)\, U + (T + ZC'Z)\, W$$
$$0 = (T - YC'Z)U + (S + K + YC'Y)\, W$$

with $ZC'Z = Z\,[Z + 12 f(a)]\, C + V$ where M, Z and Y are diagonal matrices representing the mass ionic charge on the shell, R, S, T are matrices specifying short-range core-core, shell-shell and core-shell interactions respectively, V is the matrix describing the three-body overlap interactions and $f(a)$ is related to overlap integrals of electron wave function. U and W are the vectors describing the ionic displacements and deformations respectively.

In the earlier approaches the R, S and T elements were considered to be equal to one another. In the present investigation, we have started with n approach such that $R \neq S \neq T$[10]. That is the various interactions between the ions are treated in a more general way without making them numerically equal. The dynamical matrix of the model consists of long-range Coulomb and three-body interactions and the short range overlap repulsions. The off-diagonal elements of this matrix along the symmetry directions chain a completely new term having a significant contribution for unequal R, S and T.

The lattice dynamical calculation of high-temperature superconductors is explained using an inter ionic potential consisting of long-range Coulomb part and a short range Potential of Born-Mayer form[14-15].

$$V_{ij} = a_{ij} \exp. (-b_{ij}.\, r)$$

Where i, j label the ions and r is their separation. The parameters a_{ij} and b_{ij} are the pair potentials and the parameters Y and K determine the electronic polarizabilities. The parameters used in the present calculations are given in Table 3.1. Phonon frequencies are calculated using the force constants derived from the inter ionic potential. Following Leaner et al[16] inter-ionic pair potentials for short-range interactions can be transferred from one structure to another in similar environments. The force constants evaluated by this method are in good agreement with the evaluated values[17].

Table 3.1 : Force constants for $GmBa_2Cu_3O_7$

Interaction	a (eV)	b (Å^{-1})
Gd-O	3010	2.80
Ba-O	3225	3.55
Cu-o	1260	3220
O-O	1000	3.00

Ion	Z(|e|)	Ye|)	k(e^2|Va)
Gd	2.61	2.90	895
Ba	1.90	2.32	179
Cu	1.80	3.22	1351
O (1),O(2)	-1.81	-2.70	252
O(2),O(3)	-1.81	-2.70	252

Interaction	A(e^2/2Va)	B(e^2/2Va)
Cu-O(2)	576	-90.8
Eu-O(2)	563	-80.5
Ba-O(2)	114	-13.2
O(3)-O(2)	62	-7.5

Result and Discussion

Lattice Dynamical Calculation using Shell Model ((GdBa$_2$Cu$_3$O$_7$)

The Lattice Dynamical calculations based on modified TSM

Table 3.2 : Calculated Phonon Frequency of $GdBa_2Cu_3O_7$)
(Value in parentheses are experimental frequencies are)

Symmetry Species	Lattice dynamics Frequency (cm^{-1})
A_{1g}(Raman)	555 (550)
	436 (435)
	420 (425)
	325 (320)
	165 (162)
B_{2g}	570 (580)
	545 (550)
	470 (480)
	310 (320)
	150 (145)
B_{3g}	638 (640)
	578 (580)
	572 (565)
	290 (270)
	114 (110)
B_{1u}	648 (650)
	500 (510)
	485 (480)
	415 (420)
	275 (270)
	180 (180)
	122 (120)
B_{2u}	635 (630)
	628 (620)
E_u	580 (575)
	572 (560)
	212 (212)
	195 (180)
	118 (118)
B_{3u}	640 (635)
	576 (580)
	535 (540)
	450 (420)

reproduce the observed frequencies of Raman and infrared active modes reasonable which are given in table 3.2. The calculated frequencies are in good agreement with the available experimental values. The lowest calculated Raman active A_{1g} mode frequency at 165 cm^{-1} is due to the vibration of Gd atoms and this agrees very well with the experimental frequency at 162 cm^{-1}. Similarly the calculated Raman frequency is A_{1g} symmetry at 325 cm^{-1} and 420 cm^{-1} are due to the vibration of Ba and Cu atoms respectively and the observed frequencies at 320 cm^{-1} and 425 cm^{-1} agrees very well with the calculated frequency. The highest calculated Raman frequency 555 cm^{-1} in A_{1g} symmetry is due to the vibration of O(2) atoms which also agrees very well with the observed frequency at 550 cm^{-1}. Further we have investigated the following Zone centre frequencies of B_{2g} in the Raman active mode in the symmetry at 150 cm^{-1}, 310 cm^{-1} and 470 cm^{-1} are due to the vibration of Gd, Ba and Cu atoms respectively. The maximum vibrational frequency in B_{2g} symmetry is 570 cm^{-1} which is due to the vibration of O(3) atoms.

The lowest calculated Raman active B_{3g} mode frequency at 114 cm^{-1} is due to the vibration of Gd atoms and this agrees very well with the experimental frequency at 110 cm^{-1}. Similarly the calculated Raman frequency in B_{3g} symmetry at 290 cm^{-1} and 572 cm^{-1} are due to the vibration of Ba and Cu atoms respectively and the observed frequencies at 270 and 565 cm^{-1} agrees very well with the calculated frequency. The highest calculated Raman frequency 638 cm^{-1} in B_{3g} symmetry is due to the vibration of O(3) atoms which also agrees very well with the observed frequency at 640 cm^{-1}.

The Calculated Infrared frequency in B_{1u} symmetry at 112 cm^{-1} and 180 cm^{-1} are due to the vibrations of Gd and Ba. The frequency at 415 cm^{-1} is due to the vibration of Cu(2) atoms and its observed frequency at 420 cm^{-1} is agrees very well with calculated frequencies. Similarly the frequency at 485 cm^{-1} is due to vibration of O(1) atoms and Ca atom vibrates at 180^0 out of phase to O(1) and O(2) atoms. Its observed frequency at 480 cm^{-1} agrees very well with the calculated phonon frequency. Therefore the calculated infrared frequency 500 cm^{-1} is due to the vibration of O(2) atom where as O(1) atom vibrates at 180^0 out of phase to Cu and O(2). The highest frequency in B_{1u} symmetry is 648 cm^{-1} is due to vibration of O(3) atom and its observed frequency is 650 cm^{-1} agrees very well with the calculated frequency. The calculated Infrared frequency in B_{2u} symmetry at 628 cm^{-1} and 635 cm^{-1} are due to vibration of O(2) and O(3) atoms respectively.

The calculated infrared frequencies in E_u symmetry at 118 cm^{-1} is due to vibration of Gd atom and its observed frequency 118 cm^{-1} agrees very well with the calculated

Table 3.3 : Force constants for $SmBa_2Cu_3O_7$

Interaction	a (eV)	b ($Å^{-1}$)
Sm-O	3200	2.80
Ba-O	3202	3.55
Cu-o	1250	3.22
O-O	1000	3.00

Ion	Z(|e|)	Ye|)	k(e²|Va)
Sm	2.61	2.90	985
Ba	1.90	2.32	179
Cu	1.80	3.22	135
O (1),O(2)	–1.81	–2.70	252
O(2),O(3)	–1.81	–2.70	252

Interaction	A(e^2/2Va)	B(e^2/2Va)
Cu-O(2)	576	-90.8
Sm-O(2)	563	-80.5
Ba-O(2)	114	-13.2
O(3)-O(2)	62	-7.5

frequency. The calculated frequency at 195 cm^{-1}, 212 cm^{-1}, 572 cm^{-1} are due to the bending bond vibration and it agrees with observed frequencies at 180 cm^{-1}, 212 cm^{-1} and 560 cm^{-1} agrees very well with the calculated frequencies. To calculate frequencies at 572 cm^{-1} and 580 cm^{-1} are due to vibration of O(1) and O(3) atoms respectively performing stretching bond vibration and its observed frequency 560 cm^{-1} and 575 cm^{-1} agrees very well with the calculated phonon frequency. The observed frequencies at 580 cm^{-1} agrees very well with the phonon frequency. The calculated infrared phonon frequency in B3u symmetry at 180 cm^{-1} and 190 cm^{-1} are due to the vibration of Gd and Ba atoms. The frequency at 450 cm^{-1} is due to the vibration of Cu atom. The frequency at 535 cm^{-1} is due to the vibration of O(1) atom and its observed frequency is 540 cm^{-1}. Similarly the frequency at 576 cm^{-1} is due to the vibration of O(2) atom. Its observed frequency is 580 cm^{-1} and the highest calculated frequency at 640 cm^{-1} is due to the vibration of O(3) atoms.

Lattice Dynamical Calculation using Shell Model ($SmBa_2Cu_3O_7$)

The Lattice Dynamical calculations based on modified TSM reproduce the observed frequencies of Raman and infrared active modes reasonable which are given in table 3.4. The calculated frequencies are in good agreement with the available experimental values. The lowest calculated Raman active A_{1g} mode frequency at 140 cm^{-1} is due to the vibration of Sm atoms and this agrees very well with the experimental frequency at 115 cm^{-1}. Similarly the calculated Raman frequency is A_{1g} symmetry at 220 cm^{-1} and 420 cm^{-1} are due to the vibration of Ba and Cu(3) atoms respectively and the observed frequencies at 215 cm^{-1} and 420 cm^{-1} agrees very well with the calculated frequency. The highest calculated Raman frequency 555 cm^{-1} in A_{1g} symmetry is due to the vibration of O(2) atoms which also agrees very well with the observed frequency at 550 cm^{-1}. Further we have investigated the following Zone centre frequencies of B_{2g} in the

Table 3.4 : Calculated Phonon Frequency of $SmBa_2Cu_3O_7$ (Value in parentheses are experimental frequencies)

Symmetry Species	Lattice dynamics Frequency (cm^{-1})
A_{1g}(Raman)	555 (550)
	440 (445)
	420 (420)
	220 (215)
	140 (115)
B_{2g}	637 (630)
	587 (584)
	482 (480)
	140 (150)
	90 (80)
B_{3g}	640 (625)
	580 (570)
	560 (560)
	125 (127)
	77 (78)
B_{1u}	630 (630)
	580 (575)
	475 (480)
	420 (419)
	255 (250)
	190 (180)
	88 (80)
B_{2u}	635 (630)
	612 (610)
E_u	585 (587)
	555 (556)
	190 (180)
	172 (180)
	87 (86)
B_{3u}	650 (665)
	584 (570)
	523 (520)

Raman active mode in the symmetry at 90 cm^{-1}, 140 cm^{-1} and 482 cm^{-1} are due to the vibration of Sm, Ba and Cu atoms respectively. The maximum vibration frequency in B_{2g} symmetry is 537 cm^{-1} which is due to the vibration of O(2) atoms.

The Lattice Dynamical calculations based on modified TSM reproduce the observed frequencies of Raman and infrared active modes reasonable which are given in table 3.4. The calculated frequencies are in good agreement with the available experimental values. The lowest calculated Raman active B_{3g} mode frequency at 77 cm^{-1} is due to the vibration of Sm atoms and this agrees very well with the experimental frequency at 78 cm^{-1}. Similarly the calculated Raman frequency in B_{3g} symmetry at 125 cm^{-1} and 560 cm^{-1} are due to the vibration of Ba and Cu atoms respectively and the observed frequencies at 127 cm^{-1} and 560 cm^{-1} agrees very well with the calculated frequency. The highest calculated Raman frequency 640 cm^{-1} in B_{3g} symmetry is due to the vibration of O(3) atoms which also agrees very well with the observed frequency at 625 cm^{-1}.

The Calculated Infrared frequency in B_{1u} symmetry at 88 cm^{-1} and 190 cm^{-1} are due to the vibrations of Sm and Ba. The frequency at 420 cm^{-1} is due to the vibration of Cu atoms and its observed frequency at 419 cm^{-1} is agrees very well with calculated frequencies. Similarly the frequency at 475 cm^{-1} is due to vibration of O(1) atoms and Ca atom vibrates at 180^0 out of phase to O(1) and O(2) atoms. Its observed frequency at 480 cm^{-1} agrees very well with the calculated phonon frequency. Therefore the calculated infrared frequency 580 cm^{-1} is due to the vibration of O(2) atom where as O(1) atom vibrates at 180° out of phase to Cu and O(2). The highest frequency in B_{1u} symmetry is 648 cm^{-1} is due to vibration of O(3) atom and its observed frequency is 650 cm^{-1} agrees very well with the calculated frequency.

The calculated Infrared frequency in B_{1u} symmetry at 612 cm^{-1} and 635 cm^{-1} are due to vibration of O(2) and O(3) atoms respectively. The calculated infrared frequencies in E_u symmetry at 87 cm^{-1} is due to vibration of Sm atom and its observed frequency 86 cm^{-1} agrees very well with the calculated frequency. The calculated frequency at 172 cm^{-1}, 190 cm^{-1}, 555 cm^{-1} are due to the bending bond vibration and it agrees with observed frequencies at 180 cm^{-1}, 180 cm^{-1} and 556 cm^{-1} agrees very well with the calculated frequencies. To calculate frequencies at 585 cm^{-1} and 580 cm^{-1} are due to vibration of O(1) and O(3) atoms respectively performing stretching bond vibration and its observed frequency 587 cm^{-1} and 580 cm^{-1} agrees very well with the calculated phonon frequency. The observed frequencies at 580 cm^{-1} agrees very well with the phonon frequency. The calculated infrared phonon frequency in B_{3u} symmetry at 150 cm^{-1} and 193 cm^{-1} are due to the vibration of Sm and Ba atoms. The frequency at 463 cm^{-1} is due to the vibration of Cu atom. The frequency at 523 cm^{-1} is due to the vibration of O(1) atom and its observed frequency is 520 cm^{-1}. Similarly the frequency at 584 cm^{-1} is due to the vibration of O(2) atom. Its observed frequency is 570 cm^{-1} and the highest calculated frequency at 680 cm^{-1} is due to the vibration of O(3) atoms.

Lattice Dynamics of Superconductors $EuBa_2Cu_3O_6$ and $Tl_2Ca_3Ba_2Cu_4O_{12}$

The new high T_c materials contain numerous particles in the unit cell. Thus, in a classical approach to lattice dynamics, a large number of unknown force constants has to be specified. Much attention has been paid, from several points of view, to copper-oxide-based high T_c Superconductors with the formula $EuBa_2Cu_3O_6$ discovered by Cava et al.[12].

However, the rather limited experimental data available for most of the high T_c materials, do not even allow a complete determination of the force constants for the most important interactions. Moreover, a mere fit of force constants to measured frequencies does not necessarily lead to the proper dynamical matrix, since the eigen values alone do not completely specify the eigen value problem. For systems with many particles per unit cell, the eigen vectors obtained by a such procedure may not have a proper physical meaning. Hence, a new procedure is adopted using the Shell Model, for the calculation of lattice vibrations of $EuBa_2Cu_3O_6$ and $Tl_2Ca_3Ba_2Cu_4O_{12}$ in the framework of a Shell model, based on interatomic short and long range potentials.

The use of short range potentials, as opposed to force constants has important advantages, especially in the case of the high T_c Superconductors: Ordinarily, force constants are determined by least-square fits to measured phonon dispersion curves. In case of high-T_c Superconductors, only a limited number of infrared and Raman frequencies are available for fitting, while due to the large number of particles in the unit cell, a large number of force constants need to be determined. The eigenvectors that are calculated with such a poorly defined force constant model can be quite arbitrary because an eigenvalue problem is incompletely defined by the eigenvalues along. However, the Raman and infrared spectroscopies have been employed to study the interaction of the lattice with the superconducting electronic system.

Lattice Dynamics of $EuBa_2Cu_3O_6$ based on Shell Model

The calculation of lattice dynamical vibration frequencies of $EuBa_2Cu_3O_6$ system is performed by thee-body force shell model (TSM) calculations.

Table 3.5 : Force constants for $EuBa_2Cu_3O_6$

Parameters of the model: a, b are Born-Mayer constants: Z, Y, K, ionic charge, shell charge and on-site core-shell force constant of the ion, V_a is the volume of the unit cell.

Interaction	a (eV)	b ($Å^{-1}$)
Tl-O (Same plane)	3000	2.80
Tl-O (adj plane)	3000	3.55
Ba-O	2.90	3220
Cu-O	1260	3.35
O-O	1000	3.00

Ion	Z(|e|)	(|e|)	k(e^2|Va)
Tl	2.70	2.00	1000
Ba	2.00	2.32	207
Cu	2.00	3.22	1248
O (Cu-O) Plane	−1.90	−2.70	310
O (Tl –O) Plane	−1.93	−2.70	210
O(Ba-O) Plane	−1.93	−2.70	310 (K_{11}) 2100 (K_)

Result and Discussion

Lattice Dynamical Calculation using Shell Model ($EuBa_2Cu_3O_6$)

The Lattice Dynamical calculations based on modified TSM reproduce the observed frequencies of Raman and infrared active modes reasonable which are given in Table 3.6. The calculated frequencies are in good agreement with the available experimental values. The lowest calculated Raman active A_{1g} mode frequency at 118 cm^{-1} is due to the vibration of Eu atoms and this agrees very well with the experimental frequency at 120 cm^{-1}. Similarly the calculated Raman frequency is A_{1g} symmetry at 184 cm^{-1} and 431 cm^{-1} are due to the vibration of Ba and O(2) atoms respectively and the observed frequencies at 185 and 435 cm^{-1} agrees very well with the calculated frequency. The highest calculated Raman frequency 462 cm^{-1} in A_{1g} symmetry is due to the vibration of O(3) atoms which also agrees very well with the observed frequency at 463 cm^{-1}.

Table 3.6 : Calculated Phonon Frequency of $EuBa_2Cu_3O_6$ (Value in parentheses are experimental frequencies)

Symmetry Species	Using Normal Coordinate Analysis Frequency (cm^{-1})
A_{1g}(Raman)	118 (120)
	184 (185)
	431 (435)
	462 (463)
B_{1g}	363
E_g	80 (85)
	160 (165)
	416 (416)
	437 (437)
	515 (513)
A_{2u} (IR)	136 (138)
	162 (163)
	173 (173)
	339 (340)
	497 (496)
B_{2u}	126
E_u	103 (104)
	134 (133)
	213 (213)
	372 (372)
	415 (411)
	514(5123)

Further we have investigated the following Zone centre frequencies in the Raman active mode in the symmetry at 80, 160and 416 cm^{-1} are due to the vibration of Ba, Cu and O(1) atoms respectively. The maximum vibrational frequency in E_g symmetry is 515 cm^{-1} which is due to the vibration of O(2) atoms.

The calculated infrared frequency is A_{2u} symmetry at 136 cm^{-1} is due to the vibration of Cu(1), Ba and Tl atom whereas the atom Tl vibrates at 180^0 out of phase to Ba and Cu(1) atom and the observed frequency 138 cm^{-1} agrees very well with the experimental values. The infrared photon frequency at 162 cm^{-1} is due to the vibration of Ba and Cu (1) atoms and its experimental value is 163 cm^{-1}. The evaluated photon frequency at 173 cm^{-1} is due to the vibration of Cu (1) and O(1) atoms and its experimental values is 173 cm^{-1}. The evaluated infrared frequency at 339 cm^{-1} is due to the vibration of O(2), O(1) and Cu atoms in which O(1) atom vibrates at 180^0 out of phase to O(2) and Cu atoms. The highest evaluated phonon frequency in A_{2u} symmetry is 497 cm^{-1} which is due to the vibration of O(3) atom and its observed frequency at 496 cm^{-1} in A_{2u} symmetry modes agrees very well with each other.

The evaluated phonon frequency in B_{2u} symmetry mode at 126 cm^{-1} is due to the vibration of O(1) atoms.

The Calculated infrared phonon frequency at 103 cm^{-1} in E_u symmetry is due to the vibration of Ba and Cu(1) atoms and its experimental frequency at 104 cm^{-1} agrees very well with the evaluated values. The infrared phonon frequency at 134 cm^{-1} is due to the vibration of Cu(1) and Ba atoms and its observed frequency 133 cm^{-1} agrees very well with the calculated frequency. The infrared phonon frequency at 213 cm^{-1} is due to the vibration of O(1) atom which performs bending bond vibrations and its observed frequency 213 cm^{-1} agrees very well with the calculated frequency. The highest infrared frequency 514 cm^{-1} is due to stretching of O(1) atoms and its experimental values 513 cm^{-1} agrees very well with observed frequency.

Lattice Dynamics of $Tl_2Ca_3Ba_2Cu_4O_{12}$ based on the Shell Model

The calculation of lattice dynamical vibration frequencies of $Tl_2Ca_3Ba_2Cu_4O_{12}$ system is performed by thee-body force shell model (TSM) calculations.

Table 3.7 : Parameters of the model: a, b are Born-Mayer cons-tants: Z,Y,K, ionic charge, shell charge and on-site core-shell force constant of the ion, V_a is the volume of the unit cell

Interaction	a (eV)	b (Å^{-1})
Eu-O (Same plane)	3000	2.80
EuO (adj plane)	3000	3.55
Ba-O	2.90	3220
Cu-O	1260	3.35
O-O	1000	3.00
Ca - O	2510	3.10

Ion	Z(|e|)	(|e|)	k(e^2|Va)
Eu	2.70	2.00	1000
Ba	2.00	2.32	207
Cu	2.00	3.22	1248
O (Cu-O) Plane	–1.90	–2.70	310
O (Tl -O) Plane	–1.93	–2.70	210
O(Ba-O) Plane	–1.93	–2.70	310 (II)

Result and Discussion

Lattice Dynamical Calculation using Shell Model ($Tl_2Ca_3Ba_2Cu_4O_{12}$)

The Lattice Dynamical calculations based on modified TSM reproduce the observed frequencies of Raman and infrared active modes reasonable which are given in Table 3.8. The calculated frequencies are in good agreement with the available experimental values. The lowest calculated Raman active A_{1g} mode frequency at 101 cm^{-1} is due to the vibration of Ba atoms and this agrees very well with the experimental frequency at 104 cm^{-1}. Similarly the calculated Raman frequency in A_{1g} symmetry at 126 cm^{-1} and 449 cm^{-1} are due to the vibration of Tl and O(1) atoms respectively and the observed frequencies at 127 and 459 cm^{-1} agrees very well with the calculated frequency. The highest calculated Raman

Table 3.8 : Calculated Phonon Frequency of $Tl_2Ca_3Ba_2Cu_4O_{12}$ (Value in parentheses are experimental frequencies)

Symmetry Species	Frequency (cm^{-1}) Using Lattice Dynamics
A_{1g}(Raman)	101 (104)
	126 (121)
	148 (142)
	256 (256)
	370 (360)
	449 (439)
	528 (528)
B_{1g}	206
	298
E_g	68 (65)
	107 (107)
	125 (125)
	244 (245)
	365 (365)
	378 (400)
	399 (410)
	545 (545)
	555 (567)
A_{2u} (IR)	79 (79)
	139 (137)
	143 (143)
	160 (167)
	295 (313)
	422 (432)
	432 (437)
	456 (450)
	570 (574)
B2u	126
	284
Eu	68 (68)
	107 (107)
	132 (133)
	247 (247)
	255 (255)
	355 (360)
	375 (372)
	380 (380)
	455 (455)
	559 (559)
	568 (568)

frequency 528 cm^{-1} in A_{1g} symmetry is due to the vibration of O(2) atoms which also agrees very well with the observed frequency at 528 cm^{-1}.

The Raman Phonon frequency at 206 and 298 cm^{-1} in B_{1g} symmetry are due to the vibration of O(1) and O(4) atoms respectively.

The calculated Raman Phonon frequency in E_g symmetry at 68 cm^{-1}, 244 cm^{-1}, 399 cm^{-1}, 545 cm^{-1} are due to the vibration of Ba_1, Cu_1, O(2) and O(3) atoms respectively and it agrees very well with the observed frequencies at 65 cm^{-1}, 245 cm^{-1}, 400 cm^{-1} and 545 cm^{-1} respectively.

The phonon frequencies at 107cm^{-1} is due to the vibration of Ba, Ca and Cu. The Ca and Cu vibrates at 180^0 out of phase to Ba atom. Similarly the calculated phonon frequency at 365 cm^{-1} is due to the vibration of O(4) atom, which is out of phase to O(1) atom and its observed frequency at 365 cm^{-1} agrees very well with the calculated phonon frequencies. The calculated Raman phonon frequency at 398 cm^{-1} is due the vibration due to the O(1) atom and it performs bending bond vibration in the O(4) atom and Ca atom is out of phase to O(1) and O(4) atom. The observed frequencies at 398 cm^{-1} agrees very well with the calculated phonon frequencies. The highest phonon frequencies in symmetry E_g is due to the vibration of O(4) atom and performing stretching bond vibration.

The Calculated IR frequency in A_{2u} symmetry at 79 cm^{-1} and 143 cm^{-1} are due to the vibrations of Cu(1) and Cu(2). The frequencies at 139 cm^{-1} is due to the vibration of Tl and Ba atom. The frequency at 167 cm^{-1} is due to the vibration of Ca, O(1) and O(4) atoms and its observed frequency at 157 cm^{-1} is agrees very well with calculated frequencies. Similarly the frequency at 295 cm^{-1} is due to vibration of O(1) and O(2) and Ca atoms and Ca atom vibrates at 180^0 out of phase to O(1) and O(2) atoms. Its observed frequency at 313 cm^{-1} agrees very well with the calculated phonon frequency. Therefore the calculated infrared frequency 456 cm^{-1} is due to the vibration of Ca, O(1) and O(2) atom where as O(1) atom vibrates at 180^0 out of phase to Cu and O(2). The highest frequency in A_{2u} symmetry is 570 cm^{-1} is due to vibration of O(3) atom and its observed frequency is 574 cm^{-1} agrees very well with the calculated frequency.

The calculated Infrared frequency in B_{2u} symmetry at 126 cm^{-1} and 284 cm^{-1} are due to vibration of O(1) and O(4) atoms respectively.

The calculated infrared frequencies in E_u symmetry at 68 cm^{-1} is due to vibration of Tl atom and its observed frequency 68 cm^{-1} agrees very well with the calculated frequency. The calculated frequency at 247 cm^{-1}, 375 cm^{-1}, 380 cm^{-1} are due to the bending bond vibration and it agrees with observed frequencies at 247 cm^{-1}, 372 cm^{-1} and 380 cm^{-1} agrees very well with the calculated frequencies. To calculate frequencies at 559 cm^{-1} and 568 cm^{-1} are due to vibration of O(1) and O(4) atoms respectively performing stretching bond vibration and its observed frequency 559 cm^{-1} and 568 cm^{-1} agrees very well with the calculated phonon frequency. The observed frequencies at 565 cm^{-1} agrees very well with the phonon frequency.

Lattice Dynamics of $Tl_2Ca_3Ba_2Cu_4O_{11}$ based on the Shell Model

The calculation of lattice dynamical vibration frequencies of

Table 3.9 : Parameters of the model: *a, b* are Born-Mayer constants: Z, Y, K, ionic charge, shell charge and on-site core-shell force constant of the ion, V_a is the volume of the unit cell.

Interaction	A (eV)	b (Å^{-1})
Tl-O (Same plane)	3000	2.80
Tl-O (adj plane)	3000	3.55
Ba-O	3220	2.90
Cu-O	1260	3.35
O-O	1000	3.00
Ca - O	2510	3.10

Ion	Z(|e|)	(|e|)	k(e²|Va)
Tl	2.70	2.00	1000
Ba	2.00	2.32	207
Ca	2.02	-0.50	1350
Cu	2.00	3.22	1248
O (Cu-O) Plane	-1.90	-2.70	310
O (Tl -O) Plane	-1.93	-2.70	210
O(Ba-O) Plane	-1.93	-2.70	310 (II)

$Tl_2Ca_3Ba_2Cu_4O_{11}$ system is performed by thee-body force shell model (TSM) calculations.

Result and Discussion

Lattice Dynamical Calculation using Shell Model ($Tl_2Ca_3Ba_2Cu_4O_{11}$)

The Lattice Dynamical calculations based on modified TSM reproduce the observed frequencies of Raman and infrared active modes reasonable which are given in table 3.10. The calculated frequencies are in good agreement with the available experimental values. The lowest calculated Raman active A_{1g} mode frequency at 101 cm^{-1} is due to the vibration of Ba atoms and this agrees very well with the experimental frequency at 104 cm^{-1}. Similarly the calculated Raman frequency in A_{1g} symmetry at 126 cm^{-1} and 449 cm^{-1} are due to the vibration of Tl and O(1) atoms respectively and the observed frequencies at 127 and 459 cm^{-1} agrees very well with the calculated frequency. The highest calculated Raman frequency 528 cm^{-1} in A_{1g} symmetry is due to the vibration of O(2) atoms which also agrees very well with the observed frequency at 528 cm^{-1}.

The Raman Phonon frequency at 206 and 298 cm^{-1} in B_{1g} symmetry are due to the vibration of O(1) and O(4) atoms respectively.

The calculated Raman Phonon frequency in E_g symmetry at 68 cm^{-1} 244 cm^{-1}, 399 cm^{-1}, 545 cm^{-1} are due to the vibration

Table 3.10 : Calculated Phonon Frequency of $TlCa_3Ba_2Cu_4O_{11}$ (Value in parentheses are experimental frequencies)

Symmetry Species	Frequency (cm^{-1}) Using Lattice Dynamics
A_{1g}(Raman)	101 (104)
	126 (121)
	148 (142)
	256 (256)
	370 (360)
	449 (439)
	528 (528)
B_{1g}	206
	298
E_g	68 (65)
	107 (107)
	125 (125)
	244 (245)
	365 (365)
	378 (400)
	399 (410)
	545 (545)
	555 (567)
A_{2u} (IR)	79 (79)
	139 (137)
	143 (143)
	160 (167)
	295 (313)
	422 (432)
	432 (437)
	456 (450)
	570 (574)
B_{2u}	126
	284
E_u	68 (68)
	107 (107)
	132 (133)
	247 (247)
	255 (255)
	355 (360)
	375 (372)
	380 (380)
	455 (455)
	559 (559)
	568 (568)

of Ba_1, Cu_1 , O(2) and O(3) atoms respectively and it agrees very well with the observed frequencies at 65 cm^{-1}, 245 cm^{-1}, 400 cm^{-1} and 545 cm^{-1} respectively.

The phonon frequencies at 107 cm^{-1} is due to the vibration of Ba, Ca and Cu. The Ca and Cu vibrates at 180^0 out of phase to Ba atom. Similarly the calculated phonon frequency at 365 cm^{-1} is due to the vibration of O(4) atom, which is out of phase to O(1) atom and its observed frequency at 365 cm^{-1} agrees very well with the calculated phonon frequencies. The calculated Raman phonon frequency at 398 cm^{-1} is due the vibration due to the O(1) atom and it performs bending bond vibration in the O(4) atom and Ca atom is out of phase to O(1) and O(4) atom. The observed frequencies at 398 cm^{-1} agrees very well with the calculated phonon frequencies. The highest phonon frequencies in symmetry E_g is due to the vibration of O(4) atom and performing stretching bond vibration.

The Calculated IR frequency in A_{2u} symmetry at 79 cm^{-1} and 143 cm^{-1} are due to the vibrations of Cu(1) and Cu(2). The frequencies at 139 cm^{-1} is due to the vibration of Tl and Ba atom. The frequency at 167 cm^{-1} is due to the vibration of Ca, O(1) and O(4) atoms and its observed frequency at 157 cm^{-1} is agrees very well with calculated frequencies. Similarly the frequency at 295 cm^{-1} is due to vibration of O(1) and O(2) and Ca atoms and Ca atom vibrates at 180^0 out of phase to O(1) and O(2) atoms. Its observed frequency at 313 cm^{-1} agrees very well with the calculated phonon frequency. Therefore the calculated infrared frequency 456 cm^{-1} is due to the vibration of Ca, O(1) and O(2) atom whereas O(1) atom vibrates at 180^0 out of phase to Cu and O(2). The highest frequency in A_{2u} symmetry is 570 cm^{-1} is due to vibration of O(3) atom and its observed frequency is 574 cm^{-1} agrees very well with the calculated frequency.

The calculated Infrared frequency in B_{2u} symmetry at 126 cm^{-1} and 284 cm^{-1} are due to vibration of O(1) and O(4) atoms respectively.

The calculated infrared frequencies in E_u symmetry at 68 cm^{-1} is due to vibration of Tl atom and its observed frequency 68 cm^{-1} agrees very well with the calculated frequency. The calculated frequency at 247 cm^{-1}, 375 cm^{-1}, 380 cm^{-1} are due to the bending bond vibration and it agrees with observed frequencies at 247 cm^{-1}, 372 cm^{-1} and 380 cm^{-1} agrees very well with the calculated frequencies. To calculate frequencies at 559 cm^{-1} and 568 cm^{-1} are due to vibration of O(1) and O(4) atoms respectively performing stretching bond vibration and its observed frequency 559 cm^{-1} and 568 cm^{-1} agrees very well with the calculated phonon frequency. The observed frequencies at 565 cm^{-1} agrees very well with the phonon frequency.

Lattice Dynamics of $Tl_2Ba_2CuO_6$ based on the Shell Model

The calculation of lattice dynamical vibration frequencies of $Tl_2Ba_2CuO_6$ system is performed by thee-body force shell model (TSM) calculations.

Table 3.11 : Force constants for $Tl_2Ba_2Cu_1O_6$

Parameters of the model : *a, b* are Born-Mayer constants: Z,Y,K, ionic charge, shell charge and on-site core-shell force constant of the ion, V_a is the volume of the unit cell.

Interaction	A (eV)	b (Å^{-1})
Tl-O (Same plane)	3000	2.80
Tl-O (adj plane)	3000	3.55
Ba-O	3220	2.90
Cu-O	1260	3.35
O-O	1000	3.00

Ion	Z(|e|)	(|e|)	k(e²|Va)
Tl	2.70	2.00	1000
Ba	2.00	2.32	207
Cu	2.00	3.22	1248
O (Cu-O) Plane	−1.90	−2.70	310
O (Tl –O) Plane	−1.93	−2.70	210
O(Ba-O) Plane	−1.93	−2.70	310 ($K_{\|\|}$) 2100 (K_)

Result and Discussion

Lattice Dynamical Calculation using Shell Model ($Tl_2Ba_2CuO_6$)

The Lattice Dynamical calculations based on modified TSM reproduce the observed frequencies of Raman and infrared

Table 3.12 : Calculated Phonon Frequency of $Tl_2Ba_2Cu_1O_6$ (Value in parentheses are experimental frequencies)

Symmetry Species	Frequency (cm^{-1}) Using Lattice Dynamics
A_{1g}(Raman)	124 (125)
	153 (165)
	470 (485)
	601 (603)
E_g	100
	131
	388
	491
A_{2u} (IR)	108 (108)
	141 (143)
	335 (341)
	443 (451)
	656 (648)
B_{2u}	259
E_u	84
	162 (163)
	320 (326)
	411 (419)
A_{2u} (IR)	445 (451)
	559 (563)

active modes reasonable which are given in table 3.12. The calculated frequencies are in good agreement with the available experimental values. The lowest calculated Raman active A_{1g} mode frequency at 124 cm^{-1} is due to the vibration of Ba atoms and this agrees very well with the experimental frequency at 125 cm^{-1}. Similarly the calculated Raman frequency is A_{1g} symmetry at 153 cm^{-1} and 470 cm^{-1} are due to the vibration of Tl and O(2) atoms respectively and the observed frequencies at 165 and 485 cm^{-1} agrees very well with the calculated frequency. The highest calculated Raman frequency 601 cm^{-1} in A_{1g} symmetry is due to the vibration of O(3) atoms which also agrees very well with the observed frequency at 603 cm^{-1}.

Further we have investigated the following Zone centre frequencies in the Raman active mode in the symmetry at 100, 131 and 388 cm^{-1} are due to the vibration of Ba, Tl and O(1) atoms respectively. The maximum vibrational frequency in E_g symmetry is 491 cm^{-1} which is due to the vibration of O(2) atoms.

The calculated infrared frequency is A_{2u} symmetry at 108 cm^{-1} is due to the vibration of Cu(1), Ba and Tl atom whereas the atom Tl vibrates at 180^0 out of phase to Ba and Cu(1) atom and the observed frequency 108 cm^{-1} agrees very well with the experimental values. The infrared photon frequency at 141 cm^{-1} is due to the vibration of Ba and Cu (1) atoms and its experimental value is 143 cm^{-1}. The evaluated photon frequency at 335 cm^{-1} is due to the vibration of Cu (1) and O(1) atoms and its experimental values is 341 cm^{-1}. The evaluated infrared frequency at 443 cm^{-1} is due to the vibration of O(2), O(1) and Cu atoms in which O(1) atom vibrates at 180^0 out of phase to O(2) and Cu atoms. The highest evaluated phonon frequency in A_{2u} symmetry is 656 cm^{-1} which is due to the vibration of O(3) atom and its observed frequency at 648 cm^{-1} in A_{2u} symmetry modes agrees very well with each other.

The evaluated phonon frequencyin B_{2u} symmetry mode at 259 cm^{-1} is due to the vibration od O(1) atoms.

The Calculated infrared phonon frequency at 84 cm^{-1} in E_u symmetry is due to the vibration of Tl and Cu(1) atoms and its experimental frequency at 80 cm^{-1} agrees very well with the evaluated values. The infrared phonon frequency at 162 cm^{-1} is due to the vibration of Cu(1) and Ba atoms and its observed frequency 163 cm^{-1} agrees very well with the calculated frequency. The infrared phonon frequency at 320 cm^{-1} is due to the vibration of O(1) atom which performs bending bond vibrations and its observed frequency 326 cm^{-1} agrees very well with the calculated frequency. The highest infrared frequency 559 cm^{-1} is due to stretching of O(1) atoms and its experimental values 563 cm^{-1} agrees very well with observed frequency.

Lattice Dynamics of $Tl_2Ca_2Ba_2Cu_3O_{10}$ based on the Shell Model

The study of the lattice dynamics of the high-temperature superconductors is of importance not only for the overall physical characterization of these compounds but also for an assessment of the role played by the phonons i.e., the superconducting phenomenon. A lattice dynamical study requires the knowledge of the crystal structure and the particle interactions. Usually the crystal structure is determined using X-ray diffraction. For particle interactions one has to use models, which represent the characteristic of the electronic structure and its effect on ionic interaction in a relevant manner. In lattice dynamics the ionic interactions are expressed interms of force constants.

Cox et.al.1 have refined the structure of high-temperature superconductors $Tl_2Ca_2Ba_2Cu_3O_{10}$ using neutron and powder diffraction data. Raman and infrared active modes of $Tl_2Ca_2Ba_2Cu_3O_{10}$ have been calculated by Kulkarni et.al.[2] in the framework of shell models. Belosiudov et.al[3] have calculated vibrational spectrum of $Tl_2Ca_2Ba_2Cu_3O_{10}$using interatomic interactions. A high resolution neutron diffraction study on $Tl_2Ca_2Ba_2Cu_3O_{10}$ is contributed by Ogborne et.al.[4].

Table 3.13 : Parameters of the model: *a, b* are Born- Mayer constants: Z, Y, K, ionic charge, shell charge and on-site core-shell force constant of the ion, v_a is the volumeof the unit cell

Interaction	a (eV)	b (Å^{-1})
T1-O (Same plane)	3000	2.80
T1-O (adj plane)	3000	3.55
Ba-O	3220	2.90
Ca-O	2510	3.10
Cu-O	1260	3.35
O-O	1000	3.00

ion	Z(|e|)	Y(|e|)	k(e^2|v_a)
T1	2.70	2.00	1000
Ba	2.00	2.32	207
Ca	2.02	–0.50	1350
Cu	2.00	3.22	1248
O(Cu-O) plane	–1.90	–2.70	310
O(T1-O) plane	–1.93	–2.70	210
O(Ba-O) plane	–1.93	–2.70	310 ($K_{\parallel}$) 2100 ($K_{\perp}$)

In the present work we start with a more general approach in the framework of the three body-force shell model (TSM) with R # S # T to calculate the lattice dynamics frequencies. The values of the phonon frequencies calculated in this present work at zone center by the three body force shell model is in good agreement with the available Raman and infrared values. Further a normal coordinate analysis has also been attempted for the superconductor $Tl_2Ca_2Ba_2Cu_3O_{10}$ using Wilson's F-G matrix method for the confirmation of our present investigations. The vibrational frequencies and the potential energy distribution (PED) of the optically active modes are also reported.

Lattice Dynamical Calculations of $Tl_2Ca_2Ba_2Cu_3O_{10}$ using Shell Model

The Lattice Dynamical Calculations based on modified TSM reproduce the observed frequencies of Raman and infrared active modes reasonable which are given in table 3.14. The calculated frequencies are in good agreement with the available experimental values. The lowest calculated active A_{1g} mode frequency at 104 cm^{-1} is due to the vibration of Ba, Cu(1) and Cu(2) atoms and this agrees very well with the observed frequency at 99 cm^{-1}. The evaluated Raman phonon frequency at 126 cm^{-1} is due to the vibration of Tl, Ba and Cu(1) atoms and the observed frequency at 133 cm^{-1} agrees very well with the calculated frequency. Here the Tl atom is vibrating 180° out of phase to Ba and Cu(1) atoms. Similarly the calculated Raman phonon frequency at 144 cm^{-1} is due to the vibration of Cu(1), Ba and Cu(2) atoms and Ba atom is vibrating 180° out of phase of Cu(1) and Cu(2) atoms and the observed frequency at 159 cm^{-1} agrees very well with the calculated frequency. The next calculated Raman phonon frequency at 290 cm^{-1} is due to the vibration of O(1), O(4) and Ca atoms and its observed frequency is 270 cm^{-1}. The evaluated Raman phonon frequency at 401 cm^{-1} is due to the vibration of O(1), O(4) and Ca atoms and the Ca atom is vibrating 180° out of phase to O (1) and O(4) atoms and the observed frequency 407 cm^{-1} agrees very well with the calculated frequency. The evaluated phonon frequency 489 cm^{-1} is due to Vibration of O(2) atoms. The maximum evaluated Raman frequency 608 cm^{-1} is due to the vibration of O(3) atoms and the observed frequency 601 cm^{-1} agrees very well with the calculated frequency. The evaluated Raman phonon frequency 256 cm^{-1} in B_{1g} Symmetry is due to the vibration of O(1) and O (4) atoms and the observed frequency 245 cm^{-1} agrees very well with calculated frequency.

Table 3.14 : Calculated Phonon frequencies of $Tl_2Ca_2Ba_2Cu_3O_{10}$ (Values in the Parentheses are experimental frequencies)

Symmetery Species	Frequency (cm^{-1}) Using Lattice Dynamics
A_{1g}(Raman)	104 (99)
	126 (133)
	144 (159)
	290 (270)
	401 (407)
	489 (498)
	608 (601)
B_{1g}	256 (245)
E_g	66
	136
	140
	259
	375
	415
	489
	555
A_{2u}(IR)	72 (103)
	128 (131)
	150 (151)
	190 (197)
	365 (372)
	420 (421)
	444 (454)
	607 (616)
B_{2u}	133
	306
E_u	70 (70)
	101 (101)
	145 (145)
	225 (225)
	359 (359)
	387 (397)
	435 (446)
	451 (456)
	555 (556)
	569 (563)

Similarly, the evaluated Raman phonon frequency at 66 cm^{-1} in Eg symmetry is due to the vibration of Ba, Cu(1) atoms and are in plane with Ca atom. The Raman phonon frequency at 136 cm^{-1} is due to the vibration of Tl atom. The evaluated Raman frequency at 140 cm^{-1} is due to Cu(1), Ba and Ca atoms and Ba atom is vibrating 180° out of phase of Cu(1) and Ca atoms.The evaluated phonon frequency at 259 cm^{-1} is due to the bending vibration of O(1), O(4) and Ca atoms. The phonon frequency at 375 cm^{-1} due to stretching vibration of O(1) and O(4) atoms. The calculated phonon frequency 450 cm^{-1} is due to the vibration of O(2) atoms. The phonon frequency 489 cm^{-1} is due to the vibration of O(3) atom. The highest calculated phonon frequency at 555 cm^{-1} in Eg symmetry is due to the stretching vibration of O(1) atoms.

The lowest calculated infrared phonon frequency in A_{2u} symmetry at 72 cm^{-1} is due to the vibrations of C_u(1) and C_u(2) atoms and the observed frequency at 128 cm^{-1} agrees very well with the calculated frequency. The evaluated infrared phonon frequency at 103 cm^{-1} is due to the vibration of Cu(2), Cu(1) and Tl atoms in which Tl atom vibrates 180° out of phase to Cu(2) and Cu(1) atoms and the observed frequency 131 cm^{-1} agrees very well with the calculated frequency. The next evaluated infrared phonon frequency at 150 cm^{-1} is due to the vibration of Cu(2) and Cu(1) atoms and the observed frequency at 151 cm^{-1} agrees very well with the calculated frequency.

The evaluated infrared phonon frequency at 190 cm^{-1} is due to the vibration of O(4), O(1) and Ca atoms and its observed frequency 197 cm^{-1} agrees very well with the calculated phonon frequency. The next evaluated infrared phonon frequency at 365 cm^{-1} is due to the vibration of O(2), Ca and O(1) atoms. Here Ca atom is vibrating 180° out of phase to O(2) and O(1) atoms and the observed frequency at 372 cm^{-1} agrees very well with the calculated frequency. The calculated frequency at 420 cm^{-1} is due the vibration of O(4), O(2) and Ca atoms in which Ca atom vibrates 180° out of phase to O(4) and O(2) atoms and the observed frequency

421 cm^{-1} agrees very well with the calculated frequency. The next higher calculated infrared phonon frequency at 444 cm^{-1} is due to the vibration of O(2), O(1) and Ca atoms and the observed frequency at 454 cm^{-1} agrees very well with the calculated frequency. The highest calculated infrared phonon frequency in A_{2u} symmetry at 607 cm^{-1} is due to the vibration of O(3) atom and its observed frequency at 616 cm^{-1} agrees very well with the calculated frequency.

The evaluated phonon infrared frequency in B_{2u} symmetry at 133 cm^{-1} is due to the vibration of O(4) and O(1) atoms. The calculated frequency at 306 cm^{-1} is due to the vibration of O(4) and O(1) atoms.

The lowest calculated infrared phonon frequency in Eu symmetry is 70 cm^{-1} which is due to the vibration of Cu(2) and Tl atoms and the Tl atom is vibrating out of plane to Cu(2) atom and the observed frequency 70 cm^{-1} agrees very well with the calculated frequency. The calculated infrared frequency 101 cm^{-1} is due to the vibration of Tl and Cu(2) atoms and the observed frequency at 101 cm^{-1} agrees very well with the calculated phonon frequency. The evaluated infrared phonon frequency at 145 cm^{-1} is due to the vibration of Cu(1), Cu(2) and Ba atoms in which Ba atom is vibrating 180° out of phase to Cu(1) and Cu(2) atoms and the observed frequency at 145 cm^{-1} agrees very well with the calculated frequency. The calculated infrared frequency at 255 cm^{-1} is due to vibration of Cu O(4) and O(1) atoms which performs bending bond vibrations and the observed frequency at 255 cm^{-1} agrees very well with the calculated frequency. The next calculated infrared frequency at 359 cm^{-1} is due to the vibration of O(4) and O(1) atoms and the observed frequency at 359 cm^{-1} agrees very well with the calculated frequency. The calculated infrared phonon frequency at 387 cm^{-1} is due to the vibration of O(2) and O(3) atoms and the observed frequency at 397 cm^{-1} agrees very well with the calculated frequency.

The calculated infrared phonon frequency at 435 cm^{-1} is due to the vibration of Ca, O(1) and O(4) atoms. Here Ca atom vibrates 180° out of phase to O(1) and O(4) atoms and the observed frequency at 446 cm^{-1} agrees very well with the calculated frequency. The evaluated frequency at 451 cm^{-1} is due to the vibration of O(3) and O(2) atoms and the O(2) atom vibraties out of plane to O(3) atom and the observed frequency at 456 cm^{-1} agrees very well with the calculated frequency. The evaluated infrared frequency at 555 cm^{-1} is due to the vibration of O(1) atom which performs stretching

Table 3.15 : Parameters of the model: *a, b* are Born- Mayer constants: Z, Y, K, ionic charge, shell charge and on-site core-shell force constant of the ion, v_a is the volume of the unit cell

Interaction	a (eV)	b (Å^{-1})
T1-O (Same plane)	3000	2.80
T1-O (adj plane)	3000	3.55
Ba-O	3220	2.90
Ca-O	2510	3.10
Cu-O	1260	6.35
O-O	1000	3.00

ion	Z(|e|)	Y(|e|)	k(e^2|v$_a$)
T1	2.70	2.00	1000
Ba	2.00	2.32	207
Ca	2.02	–0.50	1350
Cu	2.00	3.22	1248
O(Cu-O) plane	–1.90	–2.70	310
O(T1-O) plane	–1.93	–2.70	210
O(Ba-O) plane	–1.93	–2.70	310 ($K_{\parallel}$) 2100 ($K_{\perp}$)

vibrations and the observed frequency at 556 cm^{-1} agrees very well with the calculated frequency. The highest calculated infrared frequency in Eu symmetry at 569 cm^{-1} is due to the vibration of O(4) atom performs stretching vibration and the observed frequency 563 cm^{-1} agrees very well with the calculated frequency.

Lattice Dynamical Calculations of $TlCaBa_2Cu_2O_7$ using Shell Model

The lattice dynamical calculations based on a modified TSM reproduce the observed frequencies of Raman and infrared modes reasonably which are given in Table 3.16. The calculated frequencies are in good agreement with the available experimental values. The evaluated Raman phonon frequencies 123, 137, 468, 509 cm^{-1} in A_{1g} symmetry are due to the vibration of Ba, Cu(1), O(1) and O(2) atoms respectively and its observed frequencies 120, 148, 489 and 525 cm^{-1} agrees very well with the calculated phonon frequencies further the evaluated calculated phonon frequency 296 cm^{-1} in B_{1g} symmetry is due to the vibration of O(1) atom and the observed value 278 cm^{-1} agrees very well with the calculated frequency.

The calculated phonon frequencies at 80, 138, 338, 396 and 565 cm^{-1} in Eg symmetry are due to the vibration of Ba, $C_u(1)$, Ca, O(2) and O(1) atoms respectively.

The lowest evaluated infrared frequency at 95 cm^{-1} in A_{2u} symmetry is due to the vibration of Cu(1) atom and the observed frequency at 103 cm^{-1} agrees very well with the evaluated frequency. The evaluated infrared frequency at 125 cm^{-1} is due to the vibration of Tl and Ba atoms. Here also the observed frequency at 134 cm^{-1} agrees very well with the evaluated phonon frequency. The evaluated infrared frequency at 214 cm^{-1} is due to the vibration of Cu and O(1) atoms and its observed frequency 224 cm^{-1} agrees very well with the calculated frequency. The evaluated infrared phonon frequency at 349 cm^{-1} is due to the vibration of O(2) and Ca

Table 3.16 : Calculated Phonon frequencies of $TlCaBa_2Cu_2O_7$ (Values in the Parentheses are experimental frequencies)

SymmetrySpecies	Frequency(cm^{-1}) Using Lattice Dynamics
A_{1g}(Raman)	123 (120)
	137 (148)
	468 (485)
	509 (525)
B_{1g}	296 (278)
E_g	80
	138
	338
	396
	565
A_{2u} (IR)	95 (103)
	125 (134)
	214 (224)
	349 (433)
	445 (449)
	546 (566)
B_{2u}	189
E_u	97 (97)
	124 (124)
	240 (240)
	371 (375)
	405 (419)
	448 (448)

atoms and the observed frequency 433 cm^{-1} agrees very well with the evaluated phonon frequency. The evaluated phonon frequency at 445 cm^{-1} is due to the vibrations of Ca,O(2) and O(1) atoms in which O(1) atom is 180^0 out of phase to Cu and O(2) atoms and the observed frequency at 449 cm^{-1} agrees very well with the calculated value. The highest infrared phonon frequency in A_{2u} symmetry at 546 cm^{-1} due to the vibration of O(3) atoms which agrees very well with the observed frequency at 566 cm^{-1}. The infrared phonon frequency at 189 cm^{-1} in B_{2u} symmetry is due to the vibration of O(1) atom.

The lowest infrared phonon frquency in E_u symmetry at 97 cm^{-1} is due to the vibration of Tl and Cu(1) atoms and its observed frequency at 97 cm^{-1} agrees very well with the evaluated value. The next infrared phonon frequency 124 cm^{-1} is E_u symmetry is due to the vibration of Ca, Ba and Cu(1) atoms where atom Ba is 180° out of phase to Cu and Ca atoms. Here the observed frequency 124 cm^{-1} agrees very well with the evaluated frequency. The evaluated frequency at 240 cm^{-1} is due to the vibration of Ca and O(1) atoms and the observed frequency 240 cm^{-1} is very close to the calculated frequency. Here Ca and O(1) atom performs bending bond vibration. The evaluated frequency at 371 cm^{-1} is due to the vibration of O(2) and O(3) atoms and its observed frequency at 375 cm^{-1} agrees very well with the calculated frequency.

The evaluated phonon frequency at 405 cm^{-1} is due to the vibration of Ca and O(1) atoms and Ca atom is 180° out of phase to O(1) atoms which performs bending bond vibration and the observed frequency at 419 cm^{-1} agrees very well with the calculated frequency. The evaluated infrared phonon frequency at 448 cm^{-1} is due to the vibration of O(3), Cu(1) and O(2) atoms and O(2) atoms is 180° out of phase to O(3) and Cu(1) atoms and the observed frequency at 448 cm^{-1} agrees very well with the observed frequency. The highest evaluated infrared phonon frequency 567 cm^{-1} in E_u symmetry is due to the vibration of O(1) atom which is performing

with time, while the rest will remain zero for all times. Such a situation corresponds to normal modes of vibration *i.e.,* we say that the system is vibrating in normal mode. Obviously three will be *S*, normal modes of vibration and *S* normal frequencies $ù_1$, $ù_2$, $ù_{3...}$ $ù_s$ corresponding to each normal coordinates Q_1, Q_2, ... $Q_{s.}$

The Symmetry Of Normal Vibrations

Consider a molecule containing *N* atoms. The position of each atoms is referred by specifying three coordinates (*e.g.,* the *x, y* and *z* Cartesian coordinates. Thus the total number of coordinate values is 3*N* and the molecule has 3*N* degrees of freedom since each coordinate value may be specified quite independently of the others. However, once all 3*N* coordinates have been fixed, the bond distances and bond angles of the molecule are also fixed and no further arbitrary specifications can be made. Now the molecules is free to move in three-dimensional space, as a whole, without change of shape. We can refer to such movement by noting the position of its center of gravity at any instant. Three coordinates are needed to specify the location of the center of gravity of the molecule, and so three of the displacements correspond to the translational motion of the molecules as a whole. The remaining 3*N* – 3 are non-translational internal mode of the molecule.

In general, also, the rotation of a non-linear molecule can be resolved into components about three perpendicular axes. Specification of these axes requires three degrees of freedom, and the molecule is left with 3*N* – 6 degrees of freedom. The only other motion allowed to it is internal vibration, so non-linear *N* atomic molecule can have 3*N* – 6 different internal vibrations.

Non-linear : 3*N* – 6 fundamental vibrations ...(11)

On the other hand, if the molecule is linear, three is no rotation about the bond axis; hence only two degrees of rotational freedom are required, leaving 3N – 5 degrees of vibrational freedom—one more than in the case of a non-linear molecule.

Linear : $3N - 5$ fundamental vibrations ...(12)

In both cases, since an N-atomic molecule has $N - 1$ bonds between its atoms, $N - 1$ of the vibrations are bond-stretching motions, the other $2N - 5$ (non-linear) or $2N - 4$ (linear) are bending motions. The number of normal modes is equal to the number of vibrational degrees of freedom possessed by the molecule.

For example, consider a diatomic molecule: Here $N = 2$, $3N - 5 = 1$ and thus there can be only one fundamental vibration. Consider water molecule which is a non-linear triatomic molecule, $N - 3$, $3N - 6 = 3$. It has three modes of vibration (and three modes of rotation). Each motion is described as stretching or bending depending on the nature of the change in molecular shape; CO_2 is a linear triatomic molecule, and has four modes of vibration (and only two modes of rotation). Even a middle-sized molecule such as naphthalene ($C_{10} H_8$) has 48 distinct modes of vibration.

These vibrational motions are referred to as the normal modes of vibration (or normal vibrations) of the molecule; in general a normal vibration is defined as a molecular motion in which all the atoms move in phase and with the same frequency. The normal modes have two important properties:

1. Each of the vectors representing an instantaneous atomic displacement may be regarded as the resultant of a set of three basis vectors.
2. Each of the normal modes forms a basis for or 'belongs to' and irreducible representation of the molecule.

There are many ways in which the set of basis vectors might be chosen, but only two are of interest. In the first method, separate Cartesian coordinate system are attached to each of the atoms constituting the molecule. In such coordinate systems unit vector *s* are placed along *X*, *Y* and *Z* axes. The vectors representing the displacement of the its atom can be expressed as the vector sum of the displacement coordinate x_i, y_1, z_1. Thus, all 3*N* degrees of freedom of motion of the molecule can be represented by suitable combinations of the 3*N* Cartesian displacements.

The second method of resolving the displacement vectors of the normal modes is to use the basis vectors related to the internal coordinate—the interatomic distances and interbond angles—of the molecule. Normally, we choose first the changes in interatomic distances between bonded atoms and then as many change in bond angle as are necessary to provide a set of $3N - 6$ internal displacement vectors. For example in BF_3 molecule we require 6 internal displacement vectors to represent its 6 normal modes. We may choose the changes in B-F bond distances and the changes in two of the F-B-F angels. The sixth choice could be either a change in the remaining F-B-F angle or a change in the angle between a B-F bond axis and the plane of the molecule.

Classification of Normal Vibrations

Symmetry plays an important role in the structure of the molecule. It decides which of the vibrations are permitted or executed in Raman or infrared spectra. Since molecule possess symmetry, they are classified into various groups based on symmetry elements. Each symmetry element possess a symmetry operation.

Symmetry Elements

(i) Centre of Symmetry (i) : A molecule has a center of symmetry (*i*) if by reflection at that center (inversion), the molecule is transformed into itself (or) if there exists a point within a molecule such that for every atom a straight line can be drawn through the point connecting this atom with an equivalent atom at an equal distance from the point. Then this point is called the centre of symmetry e.g., Carbon-xi-oxide and ethylene. Molecules which do possess a centre of

symmetry may or may not have an atom at the centre. It is obvious that a molecule has only one centre of symmetry.

(ii) A p-fold rotation axis of Symmetry (Cp) **:** The molecule is said to have a p-fold rotation axis of symmetry if by rotation through $360/p$ yield a configuration indistinguishable from the original one. E.g., Water molecule. Ammonia molecule. Here rotation through 180° yields $p = 2$. hence it has two-fold rotation axis of symmetry.

(iii) Plane of Symmetry (❑) : A molecule has a plane of symmetry if by reflection at that plane, the molecule is transformed into itself. In other words a plane of symmetry bisects the molecule into two equivalent parts, one part being the mirror image of the other e.g., Water molecule. A water molecule has two vertical planes of symmetry.

(iv) Improper Rotation (Sp) : A molecule has a p-fold rotation reflection axis if by rotation through $360/p$ followed by reflection at a plane perpendicular to the axis of rotation yields a configuration indistinguishable from the original one e.g. Methane molecule.

(v) Identify E or I : All molecule possess the identity element. The corresponding symmetry operation is leaving the molecule unaltered. Hence the resulting molecule cannot be distinguished from the original one.

The vibrational and rotational energies of a molecule is increased on passing IR radiation through the sample. There are two types of molecular vibrations. They are : (1) Stretching; and (2) Bending .

(i) Stretching Vibration : Here the distance between the atoms increases or decreased but the atom remain in the same bond axis. There are two types of stretching vibrations. If the vibration does not alter any of the symmetry properties of the molecule, it is said to be a symmetric vibration; on the other hand, if the vibration is such that reflection of the molecule in any plane of symmetry results in a change of sign of the displacement, it is called an antisymmetric vibration. In a diatomic molecule there is only one mode of vibration,

the bond stretch. In a polyatomic molecule there are several modes because bonds may stretch and angles may bend.

(ii) Bonding Vibrations : The atoms change their position with respect to the original bond axis. There are four types of bending vibrations. They are: (1) Scissoring in which the two atoms approach each other: (2) Rocking in which the movements of the atoms take place in the same direction; (3) Wagging in which the two atoms move up and below the plane with respect to the central atom; (4) Twisting is the type of vibration, one of the atoms moves up the plane while the other moves down the plane with respect to the central atom.

The bending vibration, v_2, is also symmetric. Rotation of the stretching motion of molecule about the axis, however, produces a vibration which is in antiphase with the original and so this motion is described as the anti-symmetric stretching mode. The presence of symmetry in a molecule simplifies the study of its modes of vibration. Infact, each of 3N-6 (or 3N-5) vibrations are symmetric or anti-symmetric with respect to any symmetry element (e.g. plane of symmetry or a center of symmetry) of the molecule. Both symmetric and anti-symmetric modes are independent in the sense that if one is excited, then it does not excite the other. They are two of the normal modes of the molecule, its independent, collective vibrational displacements.

In general, a normal mode is an independent, synchronous motion of atoms or groups of atoms that may be excited without leading to the excitation of any other normal mode. Generally, a normal mode is a composite motion of simultaneous stretching and bending of bonds. In order to be infra-red active, there must be a dipole change during the vibration and this change may take place either along the line of the symmetry axis (parallel to it)or at right angles to the line (perpendicular). Bending modes are infrared active. This vibration is referred to as the perpendicular vibration. If there is no change in the dipole moment accompanying the vibration, then that particular vibration will be inactive in the infrared spectrum. This vibration is referred to as the parallel vibration. The symmetric stretch produces no change in the dipole moment (which remains zero) so that this vibration is not infra-red active.

The normal modes of vibration of molecules are Raman active if they are accompanied by a changing polarizability. If the normal modes of vibration leave the polarizability unchanges, they are called Raman inactive. For example, consider the H_2O molecule. The polarizability ellipsoid of water molecule may be expected to decrease in size while the bonds stretch, and to increase while they compress. While undergoing the bending motion, shape of the ellipsoid changes most. Finally, in asymmetric stretching motion ν_3, both the size and shape remain approximately constant, but the direction of the major axis changes markedly. These all three vibrations involve obvious changes in atleast one aspect of the polarizability ellipsoid, and all the Raman active.

The exclusion rule also helps us to decide which modes are active :

> "If a molecule has a center of symmetry, then Raman active vibrations are infra-red inactive and vice-versa. If there is no centre of symmetry then some (but not necessarily all) vibrations may be both Raman and Infra-red active. In CO_2 molecule, symmetric stretch is Raman active; bend and asymmetric stretch are Raman inactive."

Calculation of Force Constants : Wilson's F-G Matrix Method

The direct method of evaluating vibrational frequencies of a molecule is to write down the potential and kinetic energies of the molecule in terms of its coordinates and obtain the normal modes of the molecule by the usual methods. The method is cumbersome even for simple molecules.

Wilson's group theoretical method better known as FG matrix method while simplifying the computational steps, given a better understanding and an insight in the structural parameters such as bond length and interbond angles. (The F matrix is related to the potential energy and G matrix to the kinetic energy of the molecule). F is a matrix of force constants and thus brings the potential energies of the vibrations into the equation. G is a matrix which involves the masses and certain spatial relationships of the atoms and thus brings the kinetic energies into the equation.

The Construction of the F-Matrix

Assuming that the atoms vibrate harmonically, the potential energy V of the molecule may be written as,

$$2V = \sum_{i,j} f_{i,j} I_i I_j \qquad ...(13)$$

where I_i and I_j are changes in internal coordinates, f_{ij} are force constants and $f_{ij} = f_{ij'}$. The sum extends over all values of i and j. A term such as $f_{ii}\ I_i^2$ represents the potential energy of stretching of a bond or bending of a bond angle. It is also possible to express the potential energy in terms of symmetry coordinates as follows :

$$2V = \sum_{k1} F_{kl} S_k S_l \qquad ...(14)$$

Here $F_{k,l}$ are again force constants but pertain to the vibrations described by the symmetry coordinates S_K and $S_{1.}$ If F_{Kl} could be expressed in terms of $f_{ii'}$ the solution of the secular equation becomes easy because of its symmetry factorization. The two equations of potential energy (13) and (14) can be expressed in matrix notation. Thus

$$2V = I' f I = S' FS \qquad ...(15)$$

I's are the elements of the column matrix I and S_k's are the elements of the column matrix S, and I' and S' are corresponding row matrices.

The relationship between the internal coordinates and the symmetry coordinates can be written in matrix form as,

$$S = UI \qquad ...(16)$$

Where U is a matrix which describes a linear, orthogonal transformations. Equation (16) may be rewritten as

$$I = U^{-1} S = U' S' \quad ...(17)$$

Where U' is the inverse matrix of U and we have

$$I = (U' S)' = S' U \quad ...(18)$$

So equation (15) becomes

$$(S' U) f(U' S) = S' FS$$

$$S' (U f U') S = S' FS$$

Therefore $\quad U f U' = F \quad ...(19)$

F is a symmetric square matrix of order $3N - 6$. If there are m internal coordinates and n symmetry coordinates, the U matrix will have n rows and m columns.

Construction of the *G* Matrix

The kinetic energy T of the vibrating molecule maybe written as

$$2T = \sum_{ij} (G^{-1})_{ij} 1_i j_j \quad ...(20)$$

in internal coordinate , or as

$$2\text{T} = \sum_{kl} (G^{-1})_{ij} S_i S_l \quad ...(21)$$

in symmetry coordinate

The G matrix may be set up by a procedure similar to that used for the F matrix and we have

$$G = U gU' \quad ...(22)$$

The secular equation for the harmonic vibration of a molecule may be set up with the help of F and G matrices [15]. The frequencies of the normal vibrations are given by sovling the secular equation which is of the form

$$| FG - E \ddot{e} | = 0 \quad ...(23)$$

Where E is a unit matrix and ë, which brings the frequency of vibration, v, into the equation, is defined by

$$ë = 4\pi^2 C^2 \nu^2 \quad ...(24)$$

We define ë as $4\pi^2 \nu^2$ where ν is in Sec^{-1}, or $4\pi^2 C^2 v^2$, where ν is in cm^{-1}. If the *G* elements are expressed in atomic mass units (amu), then

$$ë = \frac{4\pi^2 C^2 v^2}{N_o} \quad ...(25)$$

Where ν is in cm^{-1}

$$\tilde{o}\ (cm^{-1}) = 1303.16\ (ë)^{1/2} \quad ...(26)$$

Equation (24) may be written

$$ë = 5.8890 \times 10^{-2}\ \nu^2 \quad ...(27)$$

The force constants *f*, their combination forming the elements of the *F* matrix are critical in their values. An appropriate combination of these values picturises the force field in the molecule. Once the elements of the *F* and *G* matrices are known for the molecule in question, the determinantal equation (23) may be written out explicitly. This is the secular equation for the vibrational problem. The great virtue of the *F* and *G* matrix method is that it affords a convenient and systematic means of employing the symmetry properties of the molecules to achieve maximum factorization of the secular equation.

The Potential-Energy Distribution

When the solutions of the secular determinant have been obtained, it is necessary to assign the calculated frequencies to the various modes of motion.

Morino and Kuchitsu have shown that the potential energy distribution rather than the normalized amplitudes is a more satisfactory quantity to use in band assignments; for a vibration of frequency ν_a, associated with a normal coordinate Q_a the potential energy of the molecule is given by

$$2V = Q_a^2 \sum_{ij} F_{ij} L_{ia} L_{ja} \quad ...(28)$$

Such terms and large only when $i = j$, since the diagonal force constants F_{ij} are much greater than the off-diagonal constants F_{ij}. Consequently we need calculate only the terms of the form

$$F_{ii}\ L_{ia}^2$$

Since the normalization condition

L′FL = ë gives relations of the form

$$\sum_{ij} F_{ij} L_{ia} L_{ja} = \ddot{e}_a \qquad ...(29)$$

Neglect of cross terms gives

$$\sum_{i} F_{ii} L_{ia}^2 = \ddot{e}_a \qquad ...(30)$$

Therefore, we get a normalized potential-energy distribution, whose terms are

$$V_{ia} = \frac{F_{ii} L_{ia}^2}{\lambda_a} \qquad ...(31)$$

Where V_{ia} is the contribution of the ith symmetry coordinate to the potential energy of the vibration whose frequency is $v_{a.}$

If one term in the potential energy distribution, V_{ia}, is much greater than any of the other terms V_{ja}, V_{ka} ...., we are justified in regarding the mode V_a as a pure vibration of the ith coordinate; if two or more terms are roughly equal, we must regard the vibration as coupled.[1-18]

Normal Co-ordinate Analysis of the Zero Wave-Vector Vibration of $GdBa_2Cu_3O_7$

The study of lattice vibrations and the free carriers is important for the understanding of the physical nature of high temperature superconductors. Raman and far-infrared studies of these superconductors have contributed significantly to the understanding of new class of superconductors. Cardona and coworkers[19] studied the infrared and Raman spectra of the super conducting cuparate perovskites $MBaCu_2O_2$ (M = Nd, Er, Dy, Tm and Eu) and reported the possible origins of phonon softening and the systematic variation of phonon frequencies with the ionic radius. Here an attempt has been made to perform the normal coordinate analysis for the phonon frequencies and the form of the zero wave vector vibrations for the $GdBa_2Cu_3O_7$ superconductors.

The high T_c superconductor $GdBa_2Cu_3O_7$ System crystallizes in the body-centered tetragonal (bct) system, which belongs to the space group 14/mmm (D^{17}_{4h}) The body-centered tetragonal (bct) unit cell of $GdBa_2Cu_3O_7$ and the numbering of the atoms are shown in Fig.4.1. The 13 atoms of the unit cell yield a total of 26 optical vibrational modes. All the above calculations are made at $q = 0$. Once of B_{2u} and B_{3u} modes corresponds to acoustic vibrations with frequency ù = O. These normal modes are distributed as follows:

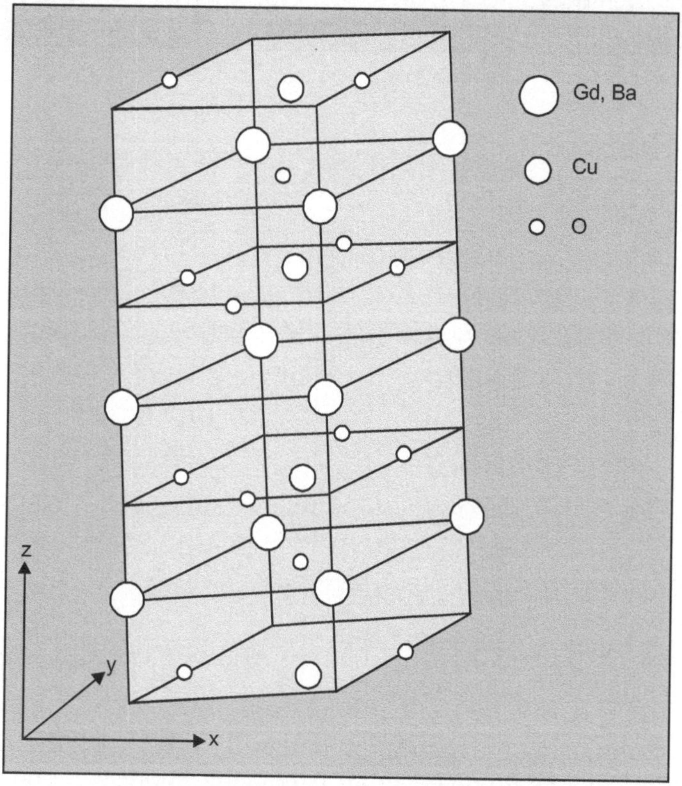

Fig. 4.1 : Crystal Structure of $GdBa_2Cu_3O_7$

$B_{1u} + B_{2u} + B_{3u} \rightarrow Gd$ atoms

$Ag + B_{2g} + B_{3g} + B_{1u} + B_{2u} + B_{3u} \rightarrow$ Ba

$Ag + B_{2g} + B_{3g} + B_{1u} + B_{2u} + B_{3u} \rightarrow$ Cu, sandwiched between Gd and Ba

$B_{1u} + B_{2u} + B_3 \rightarrow$ Cu atom surrounded by Ba atoms

$2Ag + 2B_{2g} + 2B_{3g} + 2B_{1u} + 2B_{2u} + 2B_{3u} \rightarrow$ 4O, between Gd and Ba—c axis

$Ag + B_{2g} + B_{3g} + B_{1u} + B_{2u} + B_{3u} \rightarrow$ O atom any Cu-O—b axis

$B_{1u} + B_{2u} + B_{3u} \rightarrow$ O atom Cu-O–a axis

Table 4.1 : Force constants for $GdBa_2Cu_3O_7$ (in units of 10^2 Nm^{-1} (stretching) and 10^{-18} Nm rad^{-2} (bending)

Potential Constants	Bond type	Distance(A°)	Initial value
f_a	Cu(1)-O(1)	1.94	1.4
f_b	Cu(1)-O(2)	1.82	1.6
f_c	Cu(2)-O(3)	1.93	1.4
f_d	Cu(2)-O(4)	1.96	1.4
f_e	Cu(2)-O(2)	2.33	1.1
f_g	Ba-O-(1)	2.91	0.8
f_h	Ba-O-(2)	2.75	1.0
f_k	Ba-O-(3)	2.94	0.8
f_l	Ba-O-(4)	2.94	1.0
f_m	Gd-O(3)	2.40	1.0
f_n	Gd-O(4)	2.30	0.5
f_p	Cu(2)-Cu(2)	3.37	1.3
f_α	O(1)Cu(1)-Cu(2)	—	1.3
f_β	O(3)Cu(2)-Cu(4)	—	0.5
f_γ	OCu(1)O	—	

Subtracting the translation modes $B_{1u} + B_{2u} + B_{3u}$ the $q = 0$ optical modes involved in an irreducible representation are as follows :

$$\tilde{A}_{opt} = 5A_{1g} + 5B_{2g} + 5B_{3g} + 7B_{1u} + 7B_{2u} + 7B_{3u}$$

The species belonging to A_{1g} and E_g Raman active modes whereas $A_{2u}B_u$ are infrared active modes. The A_{2u} and A_{1g} modes involve displacement along crystallographic c-axis, the B_{2u} and E_g modes along the b-axis and Eu modes along the a-axis. The normal coordinate calculation was performed using the programmes GMAT and FPERT given by Fuhrer et al[20]. The general agreement between the evaluated and observed normal frequencies of $GdBa_2Cu_3O_7$ is good. The calculated force constants using the above programmes are given in Table 4.1. It is interesting to note that the evaluated frequencies given in Table 4.2, agree favourably with the experiment values.

To check whether the chosen set of vibrational frequencies makes the maximum contribution to the potential energy associated with the normal coordinate frequencies of the super conducting material, the potential energy distributions was calculated using the equation.

$$\text{PED} = (F_{ij}\, L^2_{ik}) / \ddot{e}_k$$

Where PED is the combination of the *i*-th symmetry coordinate to the potential energy of the vibration whose frequency is $V_k F_{ij}$ are potential constants, L_{ik} are L matrix elements and $\ddot{e}_k = 4\eth^2 C^2 \nu^2_k$.

Result and Discussion of Normal Coordinate Analysis of $GdBa_2Cu_3O_7$

The G-matrix elements have been calculated from the equilibrium geometry. The initial force constants were taken from the related molecules. The final sets of potential constants provide the stability of the crystal in relation to all vibrational modes. The vibrational frequencies and potential energy distribution values are presented in this work. The potential energy distribution indicates the contribution of an individual force constant to the vibrational energy of normal modes. It clearly indicates that there is mixing of the internal displacement coordinates.

Table 4.2 : Calculated Phonon frequency of $GdBa_2Cu_3O_7$ (Values in the parentheses are experimental frequencies)

Symmetry Species	Using Normal Coordinate Analysis Frequency (cm^{-1})
A_{1g}(Raman)	560
	435
	421
	322
	160
	560
B_{2g}	530
	450
	310
	150
B_{3g}	640
	580
	572
	290
	115
B_{1u}	645
	543
	482
	415
	270
	180
	120
B_{2u}	638

The evaluated frequencies using the normal coordinate analysis method listed in table 4.2, agrees favourably with the calculated lattice dynamical frequencies and observed experimental frequencies.

The calculated Raman phonon frequency at 160 cm^{-1} in A_{1g} symmetry agrees very well with the observed frequency at 145 cm^{-1}. This is the lowest phonon frequency due to the vibration of Gd atom, and is due to the bending vibration of O(2)-Gd-O(3),which is confirmed by the potential energy distribution calculation. The calculated Raman phonon frequencies at 322 cm^{-1}, 421 cm^{-1} are due to the vibration of Ba and Cu atoms, both the oscillation are due to the bending vibrations. The highest frequency in this mode is due to the vibration of O(2). Both the frequencies agrees very well with the observed frequencies at 430 cm^{-1} and 548 cm^{-1}.

The calculated Raman phonon frequencies in B_{2g} symmetry at 150 cm^{-1}, 310 cm^{-1} and 450 cm^{-1} are due the vibration of Gd, Ba, and Cu atoms respectively. All these vibrations are bending vibration which is confirmed by the potential energy distribution calculation. The calculated phonon frequency at 560 cm^{-1} is due to the vibration of O(2) atom and it is due to stretched vibration.

The calculated Raman phonon frequencies in B_{2g} symmetry at 115 cm^{-1}, 290 cm^{-1} are due to the vibration of Gd and Ba atoms and due to the stretched vibration. The calculated phonon frequencies and observed frequencies agrees very well with each other. The Raman phonon frequencies at 572 cm^{-1}, 580 cm^{-1} and 640 cm^{-1} are due to the vibration of Cu(1)-O(2) and O(3) atoms which is due to bending vibration. The calculated infra-red phonon frequencies in B_{1u} mode at 120 cm^{-1} is due to the vibration of stretched vibration of Gd).The calculated infrared phonon frequency at 645 cm^{-1} is due to the vibration of O(4) which agrees very well with the observed phonon frequency at 640 cm^{-1} is confirmed by the Potential Energy Distribution calculation. The infrared phonon frequency at B_{2u} at 625 cm^{-1} and 638 cm^{-1} is due to the vibration of O(2) and O(4) atoms. The calculated frequency in Eu mode at 118 cm^{-1} is due to the stretched vibration of Gd. The frequencies at 180, 200 and 570 is due to the vibration of Ba,Cu and O(1) atom and the observed frequency is 170 cm^{-1}, 190 cm^{-1} and 560 cm^{-1}, the highest frequency in Eu mode is 580 cm^{-1} which is due to the vibration of O(2) atoms. This frequency is agree very well with the observed frequency 570 cm^{-1}. The frequency at B_{3u} symmetry is due to the vibration of Gd and Ba atoms. The frequencies 455 cm^{-1}, 560 cm^{-1} and 575 cm^{-1} is due to the vibration of Cu, O(1) and O(2) atoms. The higest infra-red frequency in this range is 640 cm^{-1} which is due to the vibration of O(3) atom. This frequency is agree very well with the observed frequency 640 cm^{-1}.

Normal Coordinate Analysis of the Zero Wave Vector Vibrations of $SmBa_2Cu_3O_7$

The high T_c superconductor $SmBa_2Cu_3O_7$ System crystallizes in the simple tetragonal (st) system, which belongs to the space group $P4/_{mmm}(D'_{4h})$ The simple tetragonal (st) unit cell of $SmBa_2Cu_3O_7$ and the numbering of the atoms are shown in Fig. 4.2. The 13 atoms of the unit cell yield a total of 36 optical vibrational modes. All the above calculations are made at q = 0. Once of B_{2u} and B_{3u} modes corresponds to acoustic vibrations with frequency ù = 0. These normal modes are distributed as follows :

$B_{1u} + B_{2u} + B_{3u} \rightarrow$ Sm atom

$Ag + B_{2g} + B_{3g} + B_{1u} + B_{2u} + B_{3u} \rightarrow$ Ba

$Ag + B_{2g} + B_{3g} + B_{1u} + B_{2u} + B_{3u} \rightarrow$ Cu, sandwiched between Sm and Ba

$B_{1u} + B_{2u} + B_{3u} \rightarrow$ Cu atom surrounded by Ba atoms

$2Ag + 2B_{2g} + 2B_{3g} + 2B_{1u} + 2B_{2u} + 2B_{3u} \rightarrow$ 4O, between Sm and Ba—a axis

$Ag + B_{2g} + B_{3g} + B_{1u} + B_{2u} + B_{3u} \rightarrow$ O atom any Cu-O—b axis

$B_{1u} + B_{2u} + B_{3u} \rightarrow$ O atom Cu-O–c axis

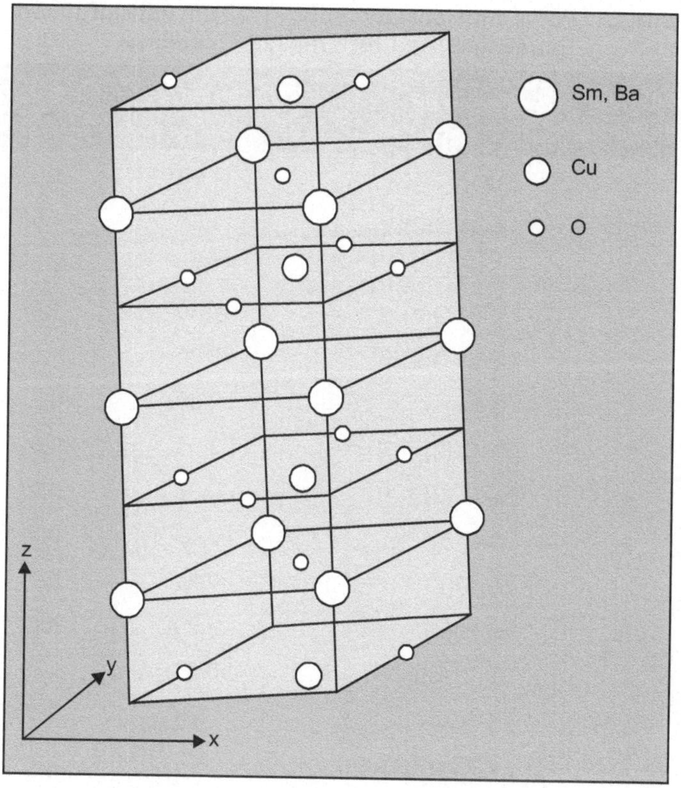

Fig. 4.2 : Crystal Structure of $SmBa_2Cu_3O_7$

Subtracting the translation modes $B_{1u} + B_{2u} + B_{3u}$ the q = 0 optical modes involved in an irreducible representation are as follows :

$$\tilde{A}_{opt} = 5A_{1g} + 5B_{2g} + 5B_{3g} + 7B_{1u} + 7B_{2u} + 7B_{3u}$$

The species belonging to A_{1g} and E_g Raman active modes whereas A_{2u} B_u are infra-red active modes. The A_{2u} and A_{1g} modes involve displacement along crystallographic c-axis, the B_{2u} and E_g modes along the b-axis and E_u modes along the a-axis. The general agreement between the evaluated and observed normal frequencies of $SmBa_2Cu_3O_7$ is good. The calculated force constants using the above programmes are given in Table 4.3. It is interesting to note that the evaluated

Table 4.3 : Force constants for $SmBa_2Cu_3O_7$ (in units of 10^2 Nm^{-1} (stretching) and 10^{-18} Nm rad^{-2} (bending)

Potential Constants	Bond type	Distance(A°)	Initial value
f_a	Cu(1)-O(1)	1.90	1.3
f_b	Cu(1)-O(2)	1.82	1.5
f_c	Cu(2)-O(3)	1.94	1.5
f_d	Cu(2)-O(4)	1.80	1.5
f_e	Cu(2)-O(2)	2.20	1.0
f_g	Ba-O-(1)	2.80	0.7
f_h	Ba-O-(2)	2.60	0.8
f_k	Ba-O-(3)	2.90	0.5
f_l	Ba-O-(4)	2.80	0.8
f_m	Sm-O(3)	2.30	0.7
f_n	Sm-O(4)	2.20	0.6
f_p	Cu(2)-Cu(2)	3.01	1.2
f_α	O(1)Cu(1)-Cu(2)		1.2
f_β	O(3)Cu(2)-Cu(4)		0.6
f_γ	OCu(1)O		

frequencies given in Table 4.4 agree favourably with the experiment values.

Table 4.4 : Calculated Phonon Frequency of $SmBa_2Cu_3O_7$ (Value in parentheses are experimental frequencies)

Symmetry Species	Using Normal Coordinate Analysis Frequency (cm^{-1})
1	2
A_{1g}(Raman)	560
	457
	436

1	2
	328
	202
B_{2g}	594
	482
	450
	235
	155
B_{3g}	600
	485
	464
	230
	135
B_{1u}	560
	490
	470
	435
	325
	250
	248
B_{2u}	597
	590
E_u	530
	478
	280

Results and Discussion of Normal Co-ordinate Analysis of $SmBa_2Cu_3O_7$

The evaluated frequencies using the normal coordinate analysis method listed in Table 4.4 agrees favorably with the calculated lattice dynamical frequencies and observed experimental frequencies.

The calculated Raman phonon frequency at 202 cm^{-1} in A_{1g} symmetry agrees very well with the observed frequency at 212 cm^{-1}. This is the lowest phonon frequency due to the vibration of Sm atom, and is due to the bending vibration of O(2)-Sm-O(3), which is confirmed by the potential energy distribution calculation. The calculated Raman phonon frequencies at 328 cm^{-1}, 436 cm^{-1} are due to the vibration of Ba and Cu atoms, both the oscillation are due to the bending vibrations. The highest frequency in this mode is due to the vibration of O(2). Both the frequencies agrees very well with the observed frequencies at 450 cm^{-1} and 548 cm^{-1}.

The calculated Raman phonon frequencies in B_{2g} symmetry at 135 cm^{-1}, 235 cm^{-1} and 450 cm^{-1} are due the vibration of Sm, Ba, and Cu atoms respectively. All these vibrations are bending vibration which is confirmed by the potential energy distribution calculation. The calculated phonon frequency at 594 cm^{-1} is due to the vibration of O(2) atom and it is due to stretched vibration.

The calculated Raman phonon frequencies in B_{2g} symmetry at 135 cm^{-1}, 230 cm^{-1} are due to the vibration of Sm and Ba atoms and due to the stretched vibration. The calculated phonon frequencies and observed frequencies agrees very well with each other. The Raman phonon frequencies at 464 cm^{-1}, 488 cm^{-1} and 600 cm^{-1} are due to the vibration of Cu(1)-O(2) and O(3) atoms which is due to bending vibration. The calculated infra-red phonon frequencies in B_{1u} mode at 248 cm^{-1} is due to the vibration of stretched vibration of Sm. The calculated infra-red phonon frequency at 560 cm^{-1} is due to the vibration of O(4) which agrees very well with the observed phonon frequency at 570 cm^{-1} is confirmed by the Potential Energy Distribution calculation. The infra-red phonon frequency at B_{2u} at 590 cm^{-1} and 597 cm^{-1} is due to the vibration of O(2) and O(4) atoms. The calculated frequency in Eu mode at 150 cm^{-1} is due to the stretched vibration of Sm. The frequencies at 220 cm^{-1}, 280 cm^{-1} and 478 cm^{-1} is due to the vibration of Ba, Cu andO (1) atom and the observed frequency is 210 cm^{-1}, 270 cm^{-1} and 438 cm^{-1}, the highest frequency in Eu mode is 530 cm^{-1} which is due to the vibration of O(2) atoms. This frequency is agree very well with the observed frequency 520 cm^{-1}. The frequency 233 cm^{-1} and 280 cm^{-1} at B_{3u} symmetry is due to the vibration of Sm and Ba atoms. The frequencies 400 cm^{-1}, 460 cm^{-1} and 511 cm^{-1} is due to the vibration of Cu,O(1) and O(2) atoms. The higest infra-red frequency in this range is 580 cm^{-1} which is due to the vibration of O(3) atom. This frequency is agree very well with the observed frequency 580 cm^{-1}.

Normal Co-ordinate Analysis of the Zero Wave-Vector Vibration of $EuBa_2Cu_3O_6$

The high T_c superconductor $EuBa_2Cu_3O_6$ System crystallizes in the body-centered tetragonal (bct) system, which belongs to the space group 14/mmm ($D^{17}{}_{4h}$) The body-centered tetragonal (bct) unit cell of $EuBa_2Cu_3O_6$ and the numbering of the atoms are shown in Fig. 4.3. The 11 atoms of the unit cell yield a total of 24 optical vibrational modes. All the above calculations are made at $q = 0$. Once of A_{2u} and E_u modes corresponds to acoustic vibrations with frequency ω = O. These normal modes are distributed as follows :

$A_{1g} + E_g + A_{2u} + E_u$	from the motion of Eu atoms
$A_{1g} + E_g + A_{2u} + E_u$	from the motion of 2 Ba atoms
$A_{2u} + E_u$	from the motion Cu (1) atoms

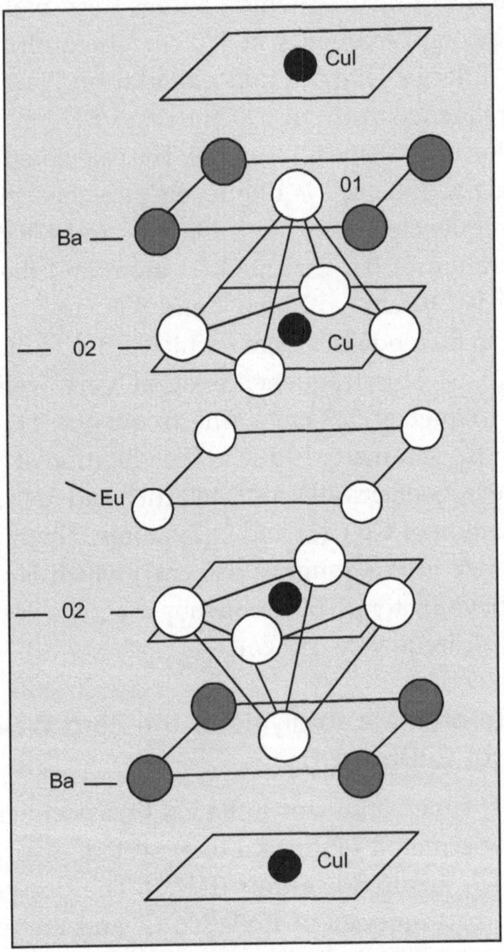

Fig. 4.3 : Unit Cell of $EuBa_2Cu_3O_6$

$E_g + A_{2u} + B_{2u} + 2E_u$	from the motion O (1) atoms alone c-axis
$A_{1g} + E_g + A_{2u} + E_u$	from the motion O (2) atoms alone b-axis
$A_{1g} + E_g + A_{2u} + E_u$	from the motion O (3) atoms alone a-axis

Subtracting the translation modes $A_{2u} + B_{2u} + E_u$ the q = 0 optical modes involved in an irreducible representation are as follows:

$$\tilde{A}_{opt} = 4A_{1g} + B_{1g} + 5E_g + 5A_{2u} + B_{2u} + 6E_u$$

The species belonging to A_{1g} and E_g Raman active modes whereas $A_{2u}B_u$ are infrared active modes.

The A_{2u} and A_{1g} modes involve displacement along crystallographic c-axis, the B_{2u} and E_g modes along the b-axis and Eu modes along the a-axis. The calculated force constants using the above programs are given in Table 4.5. It is interesting to note that the evaluated frequencies given in Table 4.6, agree favourably with the experiment values.

Table 4.5 : Force constants for $EuBa_2Cu_3O_6$ (in units of 10^2 Nm^{-1} (stretching) and 10^{-18} Nm rad^{-2} (bending))

Potential constant	bond type	distance (Å)	initial value
f_b	Ba-O(1)	2.798	0.75
f_c	Ba-O(2)	2.819	1.10
f_d	Ba-O(3)	2.851	0.81
f_e	Tl-O(1)	2.003	0.30
f_g	Tl-O(2)	2.097	0.30
f_h	Tl-O(3)	3.108	0.61
f_k	Tl-O(3)	2.402	0.48
f_l	Cu-O(1)	1.932	0.145
f_m	Cu-O(2)	2.648	1.65
f_n	Tl-O(3)-Tl	—	0.31
f_p	O(1)-Cu-O(1)	—	0.25
f_a	Tl-O(2)-Ba	—	0.46
f_β	O(2)-Tl-O(3)	—	0.80

Table 4.6 : Calculated Phonon frequency of $EuBa_2Cu_3O_6$ (Values in the parentheses are experimental frequencies)

Symmetry Species	Frequency (cm^{-1}) Using Normal Coordinate Analysis
A_{1g}(Raman)	120 (120)
	185 (185)
	437 (435)
	462 (463)
B_{1g}	363
E_g	86 (85)
	164 (165)
	420 (108)
	437 (437)
	516 (515)
A_{2u} (IR)	136 (138)
	169 (163)
	173 (173)
	339 (340)
	498 (496)
B_{2u}	126
E_u	103 (103)
	132 (133)
	214 (213)
	373 (372)
	418 (411)
	551 (513)

Result and Discussion of Normal Co-ordinate Analysis of $EuBa_2Cu_3O_6$

The evaluated frequencies using the normal coordinate analysis method listed in table 4.6 agrees favourably with the calculated lattice dynamical frequencies and observed experimental frequencies.

The calculated Raman phonon frequency at 120 cm^{-1} in A_{1g} symmetry agrees very well with the observed frequency at 120 cm^{-1}. This is the lowest phonon frequency due to the vibration of Eu atom, and is due to the bending vibration of O(2)-Cu-O(3), which is confirmed by the potential energy distribution calculation. The calculated Raman phonon frequencies at 185 cm^{-1}, 437 cm^{-1} are due to the vibration of Cu and O(2) atoms, both the oscillation are due to the bending vibrations. The highest frequency in this mode is 453 cm^{-1} is due to the vibration of O(2). Both the frequencies agrees very well with the observed frequencies at 463 cm^{-1}.

The calculated Raman phonon frequencies in E_g symmetry at 86 m^{-1}, 420 cm^{-1} and 437 cm^{-1} are due the vibration of Eu, Cu and O(2) atoms respectively. All these vibrations are bending vibration which is confirmed by the potential energy distribution calculation. The highest calculated phonon frequency at 5516 cm^{-1} is due to the vibration of (O2)atom and it is due to stretched vibration.

The calculated infra-red phonon frequencies in A_{2u} symmetry at 136 cm^{-1}, 169 cm^{-1} are due to the vibration of Cu(1) and O(1) atoms and due to the stretched vibration. The calculated phonon frequencies and observed frequencies agrees very well with each other. The infra-red phonon frequencies at 173 cm^{-1}, 339 cm^{-1} and 498 cm^{-1} are due to the vibration of Cu(1), O(2) and O(3) atoms which is due to bending vibration. The frequency at 498 cm^{-1} in this symmetry is due to the bending vibration of O(2)-Ca-O(1).

The calculated infra-red phonon frequencies in E_u mode at 103 cm^{-1} is due to the vibration of stretched vibration of Ba-O(1). The calculated highest infrared phonon frequency at 551 cm^{-1} is due to the vibration of Tl-O(3)-Tl, which agrees very well with the observed phonon frequency at 563 cm^{-1} is confirmed by the Potential Energy Distribution calculation.

Normal Coordinate Analysis of the Zero Wave Vector Vibrations of $Tl_2Ca_3Ba_2Cu_4O_{12}$

The high T_c superconductor $Tl_2Ca_3Ba_2Cu_4O_{12}$ System crystallizes in the simple tetragonal (st) system, which belongs to the space group $P4/_{mmm}(D/_{4h})$ The simple tetragonal (st)

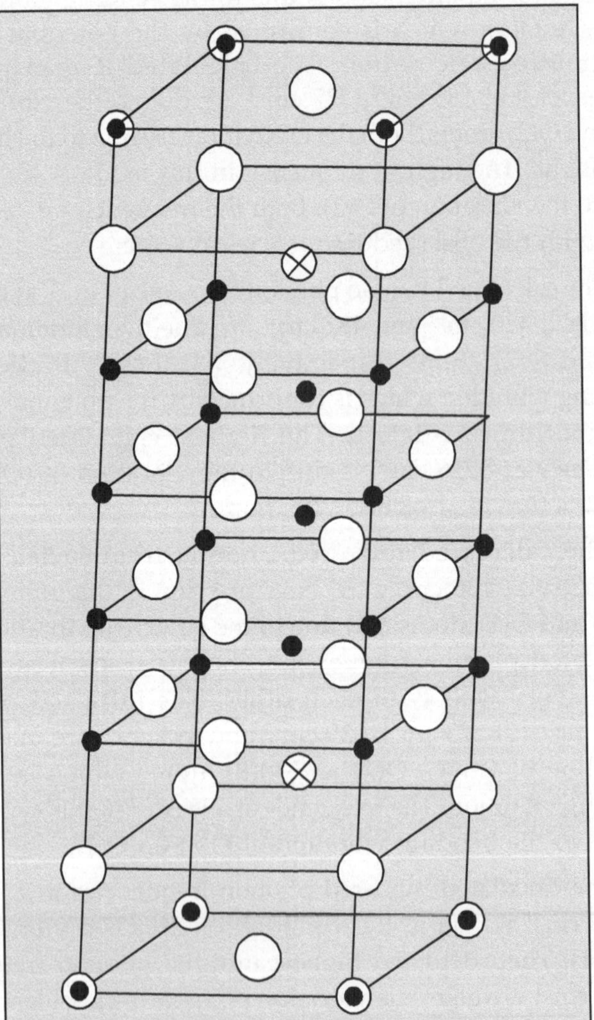

Fig. 4.4 : Unit Cell of $Tl_2Ca_3Ba_2Cu_4O_{12}$

unit cell of $Tl_2Ca_3Ba_2Cu_4O_{12}$ and the numbering of the atoms are shown in Fig. 4.4. The 21 atoms of the unit cell yield a total of 42 optical vibrational modes. All the above calculations are made at $q = 0$. Once of A_{2u} and E_u modes corresponds to acoustic vibrations with frequency $\omega = 0$. These normal modes are distributed as follows :

$A_{2u} + E_u$	from the motion of a Tl atoms
$A_{1g} + E_g + A_{2u} + E_u$	from the motion of 2Ca atoms
$A_{2u} + E_u$	from the motion of a Ca atoms
$A_{1g} + E_g + A_{2u} + E_u$	from the motion of 2Ba atoms
$2A_{1g} + 2E_g + 2A_{2u} + 2E_u$	from the motion of 4Cu atoms
$2A_{1g} + 2B_{1g} + 2E_g + 2\,A_{2u} + 2\,B_{2u} + 3E_u$	from the motion of six O(1) atoms along c-axis.
$A_{1g} + 2\,E_g + A_{2u} + B_{2u} + 2E_u$	from the motion of four O(2) atoms along b-axis
$E_g + A_{2u} + B_{2u} + E_u$	from the motion O(4) atoms along a-axis

Subtracting the translation modes $A_{2u} + B_{2u} + E_u$ the $q = 0$ optical modes involved in an irreducible representation are as follows :

$$\tilde{A}_{opt} = 7A_{1g} + 2B_{1g} + 9E_g + 10A_{2u} + 2B_{2u} + 12E_u$$

The species belonging to A_{1g} and E_g Raman active modes whereas $A_{2u}B_u$ are infra-red active modes. The A_{2u} and A_{1g} modes involve displacement along crystallographic c-axis, the B_{2u} and E_g modes along the b-axis and E_u modes along the a-axis. The general agreement between the evaluated and observed normal frequencies of $Tl_2Ca_3Ba_2Cu_4O_{12}$ is good. The calculated force constants using the above programmes are given in Table 4.7. It is interesting to note that the evaluated frequencies given in Table 4.8 agree favourably with the experiment values.

Table 4.7 : Force constants for $Tl_2Ca_3Ba_2Cu_4O_{12}$ (in units of 10^2 Nm^{-1} (stretching) and 10^{-18} Nm rad^{-2} (bending))

Potential constant	bond type	distance (Å)	initial value
f_a	Ca-O(1)	2.467	1.06
f_b	Ba-O(1)	2.798	0.75
f_c	Ba-O(2)	2.819	1.10
f_d	Ba-O(3)	2.851	0.81
f_e	Tl-O(1)	2.003	0.30
f_g	Tl-O(2)	2.097	0.30
f_h	Tl-O(3)	3.108	0.61
f_k	Tl-O(3)	2.402	0.48
f_l	Cu-O(1)	1.932	0.145
f_m	Cu-O(2)	2.648	1.65
f_n	Tl-O(3)-Tl	—	0.31
f_p	O(1)-Cu-O(1)	—	0.25
f_α	Tl-O(2)-Ba	—	0.46
f_β	O(2)-Tl-O(3)	—	0.80

Table 4.8 : Calculated Phonon Frequency of $Tl_2Ca_3Ba_2Cu_4O_{12}$ (Value in parentheses are experimental frequencies)

Symmetry Species	Frequency (cm^{-1}) Using Normal Coordinate Analysis
1	2
A_{1g}(Raman)	107 (104)
	124 (127)

1	2
	147 (142)
	256 (256)
	377 (369)
	438 (439)
	530 (528)
B_{1g}	210
	296
E_g	60 (65)
	110 (107)
	125 (125)
	240 (245)
	370 (365)
	390 (400)
	405 (410)
	550 (545)
	560 (567)
A_{2u} (IR)	80 (79)
	136 (137)
	150 (143)
	165 (167)
	300 (313)
	430 (432)
	440 (432)
	450 (450)
	580 (574)
B_{2u}	130
	283
E_u	70 (68)
	110 (107)
	134 (133)
	247 (247)
	250 (255)
	365 (360)
	378 (372)
	381 (380)
	460 (455)
	562 (559)
	570 (568)

Results and Discussion Normal Co-ordinate Analysis of $Tl_2Ca_3Ba_2Cu_4O_{12}$

The evaluated frequencies using the normal coordinate analysis method listed in table 4.8 agrees favourably with the calculated lattice dynamical frequencies and observed experimental frequencies.

The calculated Raman phonon frequency in A_{1g} symmetry at 107 cm^{-1} is due to the vibration of Ba atom which is the lowest frequency in this mode due to the stretched vibration of Ba-O(2). The calculated frequency at 124 cm^{-1} is due to the vibration of Tl atom which is due to the stretched vibration of Cu-O(1). The frequency at 147 cm^{-1} is due to the vibration of O(1)-Cu-O(1). Similarly the highest frequency in this symmetry 530 cm^{-1} is due to the vibrations of O(2) atom and it is due to the bending vibration of O(1)-Ca-O(2) which agrees very well with the observed frequency at 528 cm^{-1}, which is confirmed potential energy distribution calculation.

The frequency at 60 cm^{-1} in E_g symmertry is due the vibration of Ba atom which is due to stretched vibration of Ba-O(2). The calculated frequency at 390 cm^{-1} is due to the vibration of O(1) atom and it is due to bending vibration of Tl-O(2)-Ba. The highest frequency in this symmetry is 560 cm^{-1} is due to the vibration O(4) atom which is due to the stretched vibration. This frequency agrees very well with the observed frequency at 567 cm^{-1} which is confirmed by potential energy distribution calculation.

The lowest frequency in the A_{2u} symmetry is 80 cm^{-1} is due to the vibration of Cu(1) atom which is due to the bending vibration Tl-O(3)-Tl. The calculated frequency at 300 cm^{-1} is due to the vibration of O(2) atom which is due to the bending vibration O(1)-Cu-O(1). The highest calculated frequency in this symmetry is 588 cm^{-1}, which is due to the vibration of O(3) atom which performs stretched vibration of Ca-O(1). The calculated frequency agrees very well with the calculated frequencies is confirmed by potential energy distribution calculation.

The calculated frequency in E_u symmetry at 70 cm^{-1} is due to the vibration of Cu(2) atom and which is due to bending vibration of O(2)-Tl-O(3). The frequency at 365 cm^{-1} is due to the vibration of O(1) atom and which is due to the bending vibration. The highest calculated Infra-red Raman frequency 570 cm^{-1} is due to the vibration of O(4) atom which is performed by stretched vibration of Tl-O(4).

Normal Co-ordinate Analysis of the Zero Wave Vector Vibrations of $TlCa_3Ba_2Cu_4O_{11}$

The high T_c superconductor $TlCa_3Ba_2Cu_4O_{11}$ System crystallizes in the simple tetragonal (st) system, which belongs to the space group $P4/_{mmm}(D/_{4h})$ The simple tetragonal (st) unit cell of $TlCa_3Ba_2Cu_4O_{11}$ and the numbering of the atoms are shown in Fig. 4.5. The 21 atoms of the unit cell yield a total of 42 optical vibrational modes. All the above calculations are made at $q = 0$. Once of A_{2u} and E_u modes corresponds to acoustic vibrations with frequency ù = 0. These normal modes are distributed as follows.

$A_{2u} + E_u$	from the motion of a Tl atoms
$A_{1g} + E_g + A_{2u} + E_u$	from the motion of 2 Ca atoms
$A_{2u} + E_u$	from the motion of a Ca atoms
$A_{1g} + E_g + A_{2u} + E_u$	from the motion of 2 Ba atoms
$2A_{1g} + 2E_g + 2A_{2u} + 2E_u$	from the motion of 4 Cu atoms
$2A_{1g} + 2B_{1g} + 2E_g + 2A_{2u} + 2B_{2u} + 3E_u$	from the motion of six O (1) atoms along c-axis.
$A_{1g} + 2E_g + A_{2u} + B_{2u} + 2E_u$	from the motion of four O(2) atoms along b-axis
$E_g + A_{2u} + B_{2u} + E_u$	from the motion O (4) atoms along a-axis

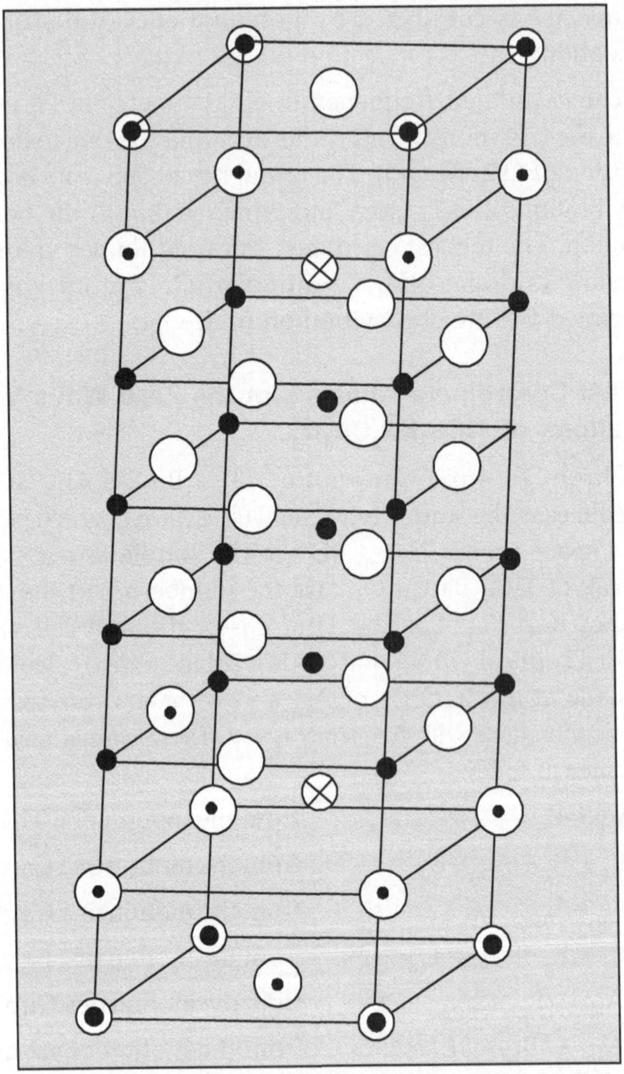

Fig. 4.5 : The Crystal Structure of $TiCa_3Ba_2Cu_4O_{11}$

Subtracting the translation modes $A_{2u} + B_{2u} + E_u$ the q = 0 optical modes involved in an irreducible representation are as follows :

$$\tilde{A}_{opt} = 7A_{1g} + 2B_{1g} + 9E_g + 10A_{2u} + 2B_{2u} + 12E_u$$

The species belonging to A_{1g} and E_g Raman active modes whereas $A_{2u}B_u$ are infra-red active modes. The A_{2u} and A_{1g} modes involve displacement along crystallographic c-axis, the B_{2u} and E_g modes along the b-axis and E_u modes along the a-axis. The calculated force constants using the above programmes are given in Table 4.9. It is interesting to note

Table 4.9 : Force constants for $TlCa_3Ba_2Cu_4O_{11}$ (in units of 10^2 Nm^{-1} (stretching) and 10^{-18} Nm rad^{-2} (bending)

Potential constant	bond type	distance (Å)	initial value
f_a	Ca-O(1)	2.467	1.06
f_b	Ba-O(1)	2.798	0.75
f_c	Ba-O(2)	2.819	1.10
f_d	Ba-O(3)	2.851	0.81
f_e	Tl-O(1)	2.003	0.30
f_g	Tl-O(2)	2.097	0.30
f_h	Tl-O(3)	3.108	0.61
f_k	Tl-O(3)	2.402	0.48
f_l	Cu-O(1)	1.932	0.145
f_m	Cu-O(2)	2.648	1.65
f_n	Tl-O(3)-Tl	—	0.31
f_p	O(1)-Cu-O(1)	—	0.25
f_α	Tl-O(2)-Ba	—	0.46
f_β	O(2)-Tl-O(3)	—	0.80

Table 4.10 : Calculated Phonon Frequency of $TlCa_3Ba_2Cu_4O_{11}$ (Value in parentheses are experimental frequencies)

Symmetry Species	Frequency (cm^{-1}) Using Normal Coordinate Analysis
1	2
A_{1g}(Raman)	107 (104)
	124 (127)

1	2
	147 (142)
	256 (256)
	377 (369)
	438 (439)
	530 (528)
B_{1g}	210
	296
E_g	60 (65)
	110 (107)
	125 (125)
	240 (245)
	370 (365)
	390 (400)
	405 (410)
	550 (545)
	560 (567)
A_{2u} (IR)	80 (79)
	136 (137)
	150 (143)
	165 (167)
	300 (313)
	430 (432)
	440 (432)
	450 (450)
	580 (574)
B_{2u}	130
	283
E_u	70 (68)
	110 (107)
	134 (133)
	247 (247)
	250 (255)
	365 (360)
	378 (372)
	381 (380)
	460 (455)
	562 (559)
	570 (568)

that the evaluated frequencies given in Table 4.10, agree favourably with the experiment values.

Results and Discussion of Normal Co-ordinate Analysis of $TlCa_3Ba_2Cu_4O_{11}$

The evaluated frequencies using the normal coordinate analysis method listed in table 4.10 agrees favourably with the calculated lattice dynamical frequencies and observed experimental frequencies.

The calculated Raman phonon frequency in A_{1g} symmetry at 107 cm^{-1} is due to the vibration of Ba atom which is the lowest frequency in this mode due to the stretched vibration of Ba-O(2). The calculated frequency at 124 cm^{-1} is due to the vibration of Tl atom which is due to the stretched vibration of Cu-O(1). The frequency at 147 cm^{-1} is due to the vibration of O(1)-Cu-O(1). Similarly the highest frequency in this symmetry 530 cm^{-1} is due to the vibrations of O(2) atom and it is due to the bending vibration of O(1)-Ca-O(2) which agrees very well with the observed frequency at 528 cm^{-1}, which is confirmed potential energy distribution calculation.

The frequency at 60 cm^{-1} in E_g symmertry is due the vibration of Ba atom which is due to stretched vibration of Ba-O(2). The calculated frequency at 390 cm^{-1} is due to the vibration of O(1) atom and it is due to bending vibration of Tl-O(2)-Ba. The highest frequency in this symmetry is 560 cm^{-1} is due to the vibration O(4) atom which is due to the stretched vibration. This frequency agrees very well with the observed frequency at 567 cm^{-1} which is confirmed by potential energy distribution calculation.

The lowest frequency in the A_{2u} symmetry is 80 cm^{-1} is due to the vibration of Cu(1) atom which is due to the bending vibration Tl-O(3)-Tl. The calculated frequency at 300 cm^{-1} is due to the vibration of O(2) atom which is due to the bending vibration O(1)-Cu-O(1). The highest calculated frequency in this symmetry is 588 cm^{-1}, which is due to the vibration of O(3) atom which performs stretched vibration of Ca-O(1). The calculated frequency agrees very well with the calculated frequencies is confirmed by potential energy distribution calculation.

The calculated frequency in E_u symmetry at 70 cm^{-1} is due to the vibration of Cu(2) atom and which is due to bending vibration of O(2)-Tl-O(3). The frequency at 365 cm^{-1} is due to the vibration of O(1) atom and which is due to the bending vibration. The highest calculated Infrared Raman frequency 570 cm^{-1} is due to the vibration of O(4) atom which is performed by stretched vibration of Tl-O(4).

Normal Co-ordinate Analysis of the Zero Wave-Vector Vibration of $Tl_2Ba_2Cu_1O_6$

The high T_c superconductor $Tl_2Ba_2Cu_1O_6$ System crystallizes in the body-centered tetragonal (bct) system, which belongs to the space group 14/mmm ($D^{17}{}_{4h}$) The body-centered tetragonal (bct) unit cell of $Tl_2Ba_2Cu_1O_6$ and the numbering of the atoms are shown in Fig. 4.6.

The 11 atoms of the unit cell yield a total of 22 optical vibrational modes. All the above calculations are made at q = 0. Once of A_{2u} and E_u modes corresponds to acoustic vibrations with frequency ω = O. These normal modes are distributed as follows:

$A_{1g} + E_g + A_{2u} + E_u$	from the motion of 2 Tl atoms
$A_{1g} + E_g + A_{2u} + E_u$	from the motion of 2 Ba atoms
$A_{2u} + E_u$	from the motion Cu (1) atoms
$E_g + A_{2u} + B_{2u} + 2E_u$	from the motion O (1) atoms alone c-axis
$A_{1g} + E_g + A_{2u} + E_u$	from the motion O (2) atoms alone b-axis
$A_{1g} + E_g + A_{2u} + E_u$	from the motion O (3) atoms alone a-axis

Subtracting the translation modes $A_{2u} + B_{2u} + E_u$ the $q = 0$ optical modes involved in an irreducible representation are as follows:

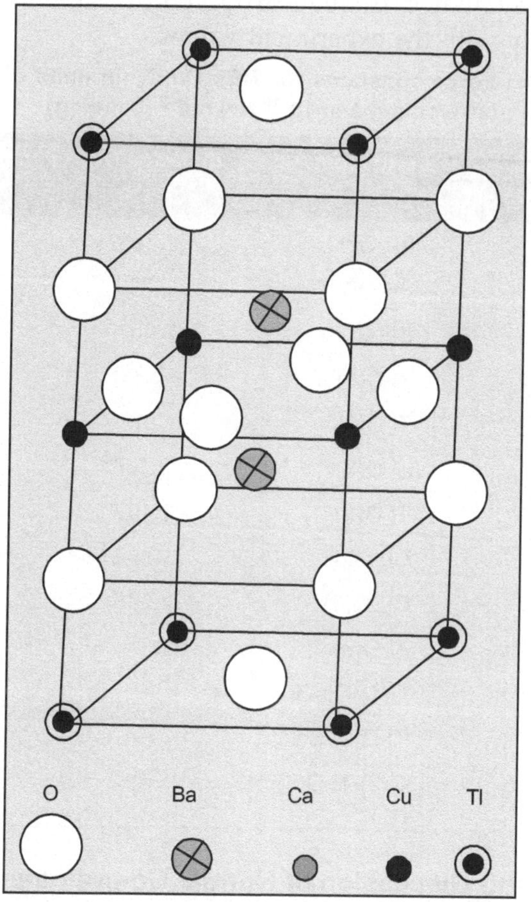

Fig. 4.6 : The Crystal Structure of $Tl_2Ba_2Cu_1O_6$

$$\tilde{A}_{opt} = 4A_{1g} + 4E_g + 6A_{2u} + B_{2u} + 7E_u$$

The species belonging to A_{1g} and E_g Raman active modes whereas $A_{2u}B_u$ are infra-red active modes. The A_{2u} and A_{1g} modes involve displacement along crystallographic c-axis, the B_{2u} and E_g modes along the b-axis and Eu modes along the a-axis. The calculated force constants using the above programmes are given in Table 4.11, It is interesting to note that the evaluated frequencies given in Table 4.12, agree favourably with the experiment values.

Table 4.11 : Force constants for $TlBa_2Cu_1O_6$ (in units of 10^2 Nm^{-1} (stretching) and 10^{-18} Nm rad^{-2} (bending)

Potential constant	bond type	distance (Å)	initial value
f_b	Ba-O(1)	2.798	0.75
f_c	Ba-O(2)	2.819	1.10
f_d	Ba-O(3)	2.851	0.81
f_e	Tl-O(1)	2.003	0.30
f_g	Tl-O(2)	2.097	0.30
f_h	Tl-O(3)	3.108	0.61
f_k	Tl-O(3)	2.402	0.48
f_l	Cu-O(1)	1.932	0.145
f_m	Cu-O(2)	2.648	1.65
f_n	Tl-O(3)-Tl	—	0.31
f_p	O(1)-Cu-O(1)	—	0.25
f_β	Tl-O(2)-Ba	—	0.46
f_β	O(2)-Tl-O(3)	—	0.80

Result and Discussion of Normal Co-ordinate Analysis of $Tl_2Ba_2Cu_1O_6$

The evaluated frequencies using the normal coordinate analysis method listed in table 4.12 agrees favourably with the calculated lattice dynamical frequencies and observed experimental frequencies.

The calculated Raman phonon frequency at 121 cm^{-1} in A_{1g} symmetry agrees very well with the observed frequency at 125 cm^{-1}. This is the lowest phonon frequency due to the vibration of Ba atom, and is due to the bending vibration of O(2)-Tl-O(3),which is confirmed by the potential energy

Table 4.12 : Calculated Phonon frequency of $TlBa_2Cu_1O_6$ (Values in the parentheses are experimental frequencies)

Symmetry Species	Frequency (cm^{-1}) Using Normal Coordinate Analysis
A_{1g}(Raman)	121 (125)
	161 (165)
	482 (485)
	602 (603)
E_g	106
	134
	400
	499
A_{2u} (IR)	115 (108)
	139 (143)
	351 (341)
	441 (451)
	641 (648)
B_{2u}	270
E_u	89
	168 (163)
	321 (326)
	406 (419)
	448 (451)
	561 (563)

distribution calculation. The calculated Raman phonon frequencies at 161 cm^{-1}, 602 cm^{-1} are due to the vibration of Tl and O(2) atoms, both the oscillation are due to the bending vibrations. The highest frequency in this mode is due to the vibration of O(2). Both the frequencies agrees very well with the observed frequencies at 165 cm^{-1} and 603 cm^{-1}.

The calculated Raman phonon frequencies in E_g symmetry at 106 cm^{-1}, 400 cm^{-1} and 499 cm^{-1} are due the vibration of Ba, Tl, and O(2) atoms respectively. All these vibrations are bending vibration which is confirmed by the potential energy distribution calculation. The calculated phonon frequency at 134cm^{-1} is due to the vibration of Tl atom and it is due to stretched vibration.

The calculated infra-red phonon frequencies in A_{2u} symmetry at 115 cm^{-1}, 351 cm^{-1} are due to the vibration of Cu(1) and O(1) atoms and due to the stretched vibration. The calculated phonon frequencies and observed frequencies agrees very well with each other. The infra-red phonon frequencies at 139 cm^{-1}, 441 cm^{-1} and 641 cm^{-1} are due to the vibration of Cu(1)-O(2) and O(3) atoms which is due to bending vibration. The frequency at 641 cm^{-1} in this symmetry is due to the bending vibration of O(2)-Ca-O(1).

The calculated infra-red phonon frequencies in E_u mode at 89 cm^{-1} is due to the vibration of stretched vibration of Ba-O(1). The calculated infra-red phonon frequency at 448 cm^{-1} is due to the vibration of Tl-O(3)-Tl, which agrees very well with the observed phonon frequency at 563 cm^{-1} is confirmed by the Potential Energy Distribution calculation.

Normal Co-ordinate Analysis of the Zero Wave Vector Vibrations of $Tl_2Ca_2Ba_2Cu_3O_{10}$

The high T_c superconductor $Tl_2Ca_2Ba_2Cu_3O_{10}$ System crystallizes in the body-centered tetragonal (bct) system which belongs to the space group $14/_{mmm}$ $(D^{17}{}_{4h})$ The body-centered tetragonal (bct) unit cell of $Tl_2Ca_2Ba_2Cu_3O_{10}$ and the numbering of the atoms are shown in Fig. 4.7. The 19 atoms of the unit cell yield a total of 38 optical vibrational modes. All of above calculations are made at $q = 0$. One of A_{2u} and E_u modes corresponds to acoustic vibrations with frequency $\varpi = 0$. These normal modes are distributed as follows:

$A_{1g} + E_g + A_{2u} + E_u$ $\rightarrow$ from the motion of 2Tl atoms

$A_{1g} + E_g + E_u$ $\rightarrow$ from the motion of 2Ba atoms

$A_{1g} + E_g + A_{2u} + E_u$	$\rightarrow$ from the motion of 2 Ca atoms
$A_{1g} + E_g + A_{2u} + E_u$	$\rightarrow$ from the motion of 2 Cu(1) atoms
$A_{2u} + E_u$	$\rightarrow$ from the motion of Cu (2) atoms
$A_{1g} + 2E_g + B_{1g} + 2A_{2u} + 2B_{2u} + 3E_u$	$\rightarrow$ from the motion of O (1) atoms along c-axis.

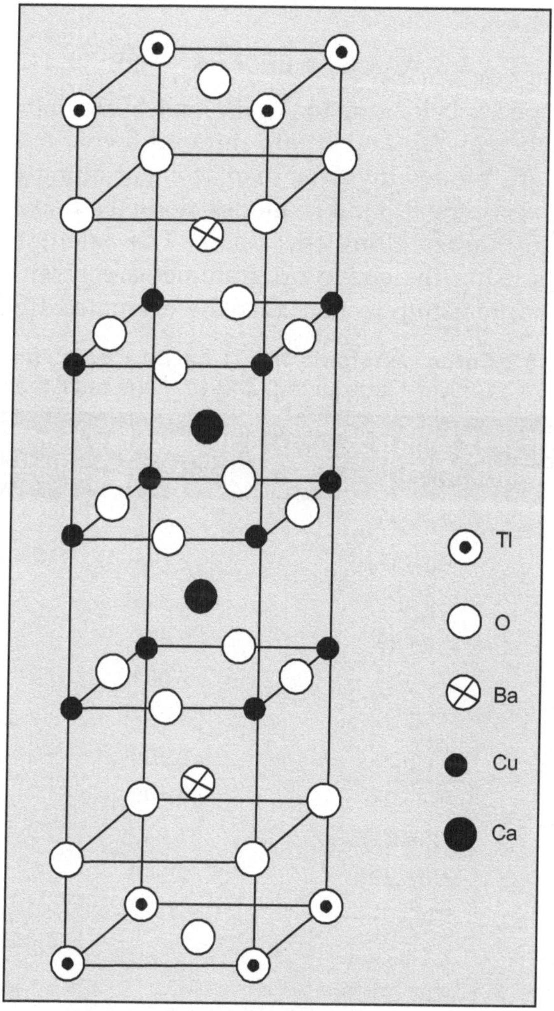

Fig. 4.7 : Unit Cell of $Tl_2Ca_2Ba_2Cu_3O_{10}$

$A_{1g} + E_{1g} + 2A_{2u} + 2E_u$ → from the motion of O(2) atoms along the b-axis.

$A_{1g} + E_g + A_{2u} + E_u$ → from the motion of O(3) atoms along the a-axis.

Subtracting the translation modes A2u + B_{2u} + E_u the $q = 0$ optical modes involved in an irreducible representation are as follows :

$$\Gamma_{opt} = 7\,A_{1g} + B_{1g} + 8E_g + 9A_{2u} + 2B_{2u} + 11E_u$$

The species belonging to A_{1g}, B_{1g} and E_g are Raman active modes whereas A_{2u} and B_u are infrared active modes. The A_{2u} and A_{1g} modes involves displacement along crystallographic c-axis, the B_{2u} and E_g modes along the b-axis and the B_{1g} and E_u modes along the a-axis. The calculated force constants using the above programmes are given in Table 4.13. It is interesting to note that the evaluated frequencies

Table 4.13 : Force constants for $Tl_2Ca_2Ba_2Cu_3O_{10}$ (in units of 10^2 Nm^{-1} (stretching) and 10^{-18} Nm rad^{-2} (bending))

Potential constant	bond type	distance (Å)	initial value
f_a	Ca-O(1)	2.467	1.06
f_b	Ba-O(1)	2.798	0.75
f_c	Ba-O(2)	2.819	1.10
f_d	Ba-O(3)	2.851	0.81
f_e	Tl-O(1)	2.003	0.30
f_g	Tl-O(2)	2.097	0.30
f_h	Tl-O(3)	3.108	0.61
f_k	Tl-O(3)	2.402	0.48
f_l	Cu-O(1)	1.932	0.145
f_m	Cu-O(2)	2.648	1.65
f_n	Tl-O(3) –Tl	—	0.31
f_p	O(1)-Cu-O(1)	—	0.25
f_α	Tl-O(2)-Ba	—	0.46
f_β	O(2)-Tl-O(3)	—	0.80

given in Table 4.14 agree favourably with the experimental values.

Table 4.14 : Calculated Phonon frequencies of $Tl_2Ca_2Ba_2Cu_3O_{10}$ (Values in the Parentheses are experimental frequencies)

Symmetry Species	Using Normal Coordinate Analysis (cm^{-1})
1	2
A_{1g}(Raman)	110
	130
	151
	281
	412
	486
	605
B_{1g}	261
E_g	70
	142
	164
	270
	365
	411
	471
	554
A_{2u}(IR)	81
	120
	148
	181
	369
	411

1	2
	449
	592
B_{2u}	138
	309
E_u	69
	105
	152
	228
	358
	390
	441
	458
	562
	571

Result and Discussion of $Tl_2Ca_2Ba_2Cu_3O_{10}$ using Normal Co-ordinate Analysis

The Normal Coordinate Analysis of $Tl_2Ca_2Ba_2Cu_3O_{10}$ reproduces the observed frequencies of Raman and infra-red active modes reasonable which are given in table 4.14. The calculated frequencies are in good agreement with the available experimental values. The lowest calculated active A_{1g} mode frequency at 110 cm^{-1} is due to the vibration of Ba, Cu(1) and Cu(2) atoms. The evaluated Raman phonon frequency at 130 cm^{-1} is due to the vibration of Tl, Ba and Cu(1) atoms. Here the Tl atom is vibrating 180° out of phase to Ba and Cu(1) atoms. Similarly the calculated Raman phonon frequency at 151 cm^{-1} is due to the vibration of Cu(1), Ba and Cu(2) atoms and Ba atom is vibrating 180° out of phase of Cu(1) and Cu(2) atoms. The next calculated Raman phonon frequency at 281 cm^{-1} is due to the vibration of O(1), O(4) and Ca atoms. The evaluated Raman phonon frequency at 412 cm^{-1} is due to the vibration of O(1), O(4) and Ca atoms and the Ca atom is vibrating 180° out of phase to O (1) and O(4) atoms. The evaluated phonon frequency 486 cm^{-1} is due to Vibration of O(2) atoms. The maximum evaluated Raman frequency 605 cm^{-1} is due to the vibration of O(3) atoms. The evaluated Raman phonon frequency 261 cm^{-1} in B_{1g} Symmetry is due to the vibration of O(1) and O (4) atoms.

Similarly, the evaluated Raman phonon frequency at 70 cm^{-1} in E_g symmetry is due to the vibration of Ba, Cu(1) atoms and are in plane with Ca atom. The Raman phonon frequency at 142 cm^{-1} is due to the vibration of Tl atom. The evaluated Raman frequency at 164 cm^{-1} is due to Cu(1), Ba and Ca atoms and Ba atom is vibrating 180° out of phase of Cu(1) and Ca atoms.The evaluated phonon frequency at 270 cm^{-1} is due to the bending vibration of O(1), O(4) and Ca atoms. The phonon frequency at 365 cm^{-1} due to stretching vibration of O(1) and O(4) atoms. The calculated phonon frequency 411 cm^{-1} is due to the vibration of O(2) atoms. The phonon frequency 471 cm^{-1} is due to the vibration of O(3) atom. The highest calculated phonon frequency at 554 cm^{-1} in E_g symmetry is due to the stretching vibration of O(1) atoms.

The lowest calculated infrared phonon frequency in A_{2u} symmetry at 81 cm^{-1} is due to the vibrations of C_u(1) and C_u(2) atoms. The evaluated infra-red phonon frequency at 120 cm^{-1} is due to the vibration of Cu(2), Cu(1) and Tl atoms in which Tl atom vibrates 180° out of phase to Cu(2) and Cu(1) atoms. The next evaluated infra-red phonon frequency at 148 cm^{-1} is due to the vibration of Cu(2) and Cu(1) atoms. The evaluated infra-red phonon frequency at 181 cm^{-1} is due to the vibration of O(4), O(1) and Ca atoms. The next evaluated infra-red phonon frequency at 369 cm^{-1} is due to the vibration of O(2), Ca and O(1) atoms. Here Ca atom is vibrating 180° out of phase to O(2) and O(1) atoms. The calculated frequency at 411 cm^{-1} is due the vibration of O(4), O(2) and Ca atoms in which Ca atom vibrates 180° out of phase to O(4) and O(2) atoms. The next higher calculated infra-red phonon frequency at 449 cm^{-1} is due to the vibration of O(2), O(1) and Ca atoms. The highest calculated infra-red phonon frequency in A_{2u} symmetry at 592 cm^{-1} is due to the vibration of O(3) atom.

The evaluated phonon infra-red frequency in B_{2u} symmetry at 138 cm^{-1} is due to the vibration of O(4) and O(1) atoms. The calculated frequency at 309 cm^{-1} is due to the vibration of O(4) and O(1) atoms.

The lowest calculated infrared phonon frequency in Eu symmetry is 69 cm^{-1} which is due to the vibration of Cu(2) and Tl atoms and the Tl atom is vibrating out of plane to Cu(2) atom. The calculated infrared frequency 105 cm^{-1} is due to the vibration of Tl and Cu(2) atoms. The evaluated infrared phonon frequency at 152 cm^{-1} is due to the vibration of Cu(1), Cu(2) and Ba atoms in which Ba atom is vibrating 180° out of phase to Cu(1) and Cu(2) atoms. The calculated infra-red frequency at 228 cm^{-1} is due to vibration of Cu O(4) and O(1) atoms which performs bending bond vibrations. The next calculated infra-red frequency at 358 cm^{-1} is due to the vibration of O(4) and O(1) atoms. The calculated infra-red phonon frequency at 390 cm^{-1} is due to the vibration of O(2) and O(3) atoms.

The calculated infra-red phonon frequency at 441 cm^{-1} is due to the vibration of Ca, O(1) and O(4) atoms. Here Ca atom vibrates 180° out of phase to O(1) and O(4) atoms. The evaluated frequency at 458 cm^{-1} is due to the vibration of O(3) and O(2) atoms and the O(2) atom vibraties out of plane to O(3) atom. The evaluated infra-red frequency at 562 cm^{-1} is due to the vibration of O(1) atom which performs stretching vibrations. The highest calculated infra-red frequency in Eu symmetry at 571 cm^{-1} is due to the vibration of O(4) atom performs stretching vibration.

Vibrational modes on the region 400-500 cm^{-1} are attributed to Ca-O(2) stretching. The present potential energy distribution confirms our conclusion. The lower frequency modes involve the small displacement of Ca-O(2) and Ba-O and the angular displacement of O-Ca-O. The evaluated frequencies using the normal coordinate analysis method listed in table 4.14 agree favourably with the calculated lattice dynamical frequencies and observed experimental frequencies.

Normal Co-ordinate Analysis of the Zero Wave Vector Vibrations of $TlCaBa_2Cu_2O_7$

The high T_c superconductor $TlCaBa_2Cu_2O_7$ System crystallizes in the simple-tetragonal (st) system which belongs to the space group $P4/_{mmm}$ (D^1_{4h}) The simple-tetragonal (st) unit cell of $TlCaBa_2Cu_2O_7$ and the numbering of the atoms are shown in Fig. 4.8. The 13 atoms of the unit cell yield a total of 26 optical vibrational modes. All of above calculations are made at $q = 0$. One of A_{2u} and E_u modes corresponds to acoustic vibrations with frequency $\varpi = 0$. These normal modes are distributed as follows.

$A_{2u} + E_u$	→ from the motion of Tl atom.
$A_{2u} + E_u$	→ from the motion of Ca atom
$A_{1g} + E_g + E_u$	→ from the motion of 2Ba atoms
$A_{1g} + E_g + A_{2u} + E_u$	→ from the motion of 2Cu(1) atom
$A_{1g} + B_{1g} + 2E_g + 2A_{2u} + B_{2u} + 2E_u$	→ from the motion of 4 O(1)along c-axis
$A_{1g} + E_g + A_{2u} + E_u$	→ from the motion of 2 O(2)atoms along b-axis
$A_{2u} + E_u$	→ from the motion of O(3)atoms along a-axis

Subtracting the translation modes $A_{2u} + B_{2u} + E_u$ the $q = 0$ optical modes involved in an irreducible representation are as follows :

$$\Gamma_{opt} = 4A_{1g} + B_{1g} + 5E_g + 7A_{2u} + B_{2u} + 8E_u$$

The species belonging to A_{1g} B_{1g} and E_g are Raman active modes whereas A_{2u} and B_u are infra-red active modes. The

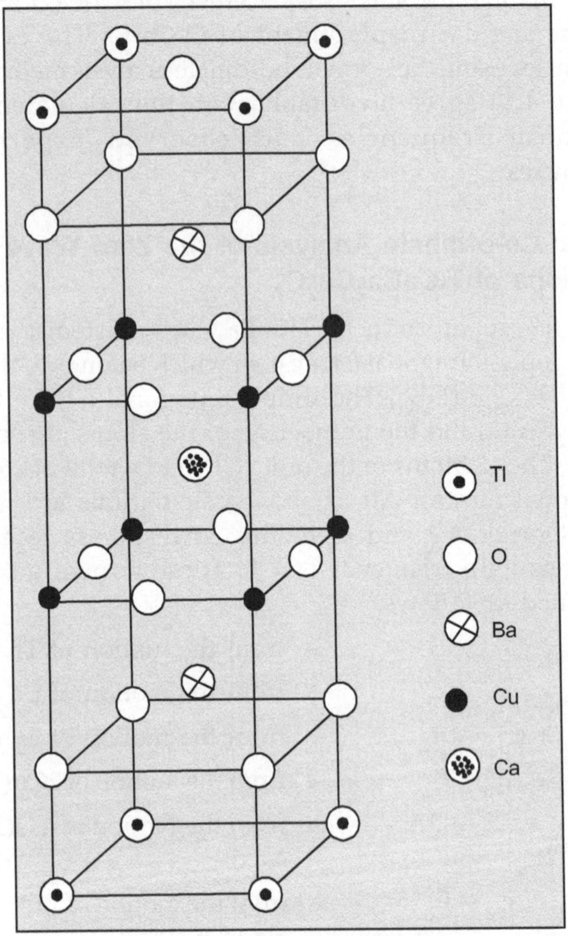

Fig. 4.8 : Unit Cell of $TiCaBa_2Cu_3O_7$

A_{2u} and A_{1g} modes involves displacement along crystallographic c-axis, the B_{2u} and E_g modes along the b-axis and the E_g and E_u modes along the a-axis The calculated force constants using the above programmes are given in Table 4.15. It is interesting to note that the evaluated frequencies given in Table 4.16 agree favourably with the experimental values.

Table 4.15. Force constants for $TlCaBa_2Cu_2O_7$ (in units of 10^2 Nm^{-1} (stretching) and 10^{-18} Nm rad^{-2} (bending)

Potential constant	bond type	distance (Å)	initial value
f_a	Ca-O(1)	2.467	1.06
f_b	Ba-O(1)	2.798	0.75
f_c	Ba-O(2)	2.819	1.10
f_d	Ba-O(3)	2.851	0.81
f_e	Tl-O(1)	2.003	0.30
f_g	Tl-O(2)	2.097	0.30
f_h	Tl-O(3)	3.108	0.61
f_k	Tl-O(3)	2.402	0.48
f_l	Cu-O(1)	1.932	0.145
f_m	Cu-O(2)	2.648	1.65
f_n	Tl-O(3) –Tl	—	0.31
f_p	O(1)-Cu-O(1)	—	0.25
f_α	Tl-O(2)-Ba	—	0.46
f_β	O(2)-Tl-O(3)	—	0.80

Results and Discussion of Normal Co-ordinate Analysis of $TlCaBa_2Cu_2O_7$

The Normal Coordinate Analysis of $TlCaBa_2Cu_2O_7$ reproduce the observed frequencies of Raman and infra-red modes reasonably which are given in Table 4.16. The evaluated Raman phonon frequencies 126, 161, 462, 498 cm^{-1} in A_{1g} symmetry are due to the vibration of Ba, Cu(1), O(1) and O(2) atoms respectively, further the evaluated calculated phonon frequency 289 cm^{-1} in B_{1g} symmetry is due to the vibration of O(1) atom.

Table 4.16. Calculated Phonon frequencies of $TlCaBa_2Cu_2O_7$ (Values in the Parentheses are experimental frequencies).

Symmetry Species	Using Normal Co-ordinate Analysis (cm^{-1})
A_{1g}(Raman)	126
	161
	462
	498
B_{1g}	289
E_g	81
	141
	342
	400
	572
A_{2u} (IR)	101
	131
	219
	345
	451
	548
B_{2u}	192
E_u	98
	131
	241
	368
	411
	449
	574

The calculated phonon frequencies at 81, 141, 342, 400 and 572 cm^{-1} in Eg symmetry are due to the vibration of Ba, $C_u(1)$, Ca, O(2) and O(1) atoms respectively.

The lowest evaluated infra-red frequency at 101 cm^{-1} in A_{2u} symmetry is due to the vibration of Cu(1) atom. The evaluated infra-red frequency at 131 cm^{-1} is due to the vibration of Tl and Ba atoms.. The evaluated infra-red frequency at 219 cm^{-1} is due to the vibration of Cu and O(1) atoms. The evaluated infra-red phonon frequency at 345 cm^{-1} is due to the vibration of O(2) and Ca. The evaluated phonon frequency at 451 cm^{-1} is due to the vibrations of Ca, O(2) and O(1) atoms in which O(1) atom is 180^0 out of phase to Cu and O(2) atoms. The highest infrared phonon frequency in A_{2u} symmetry at 548 cm^{-1} due to the vibration of O(3) atoms. The infra-red phonon frequency at 192 cm^{-1} in B_{2u} symmetry is due to the vibration of O(1) atom.

The lowest infrared phonon frquency in E_u symmetry at 98 cm^{-1} is due to the vibration of Tl and Cu(1) atoms. The next infra-red phonon frequency 131 cm^{-1} is E_u symmetry is due to the vibration of Ca, Ba and Cu(1) atoms where atom Ba is 180^0 out of phase to Cu and Ca atoms. The evaluated frequency at 241 cm^{-1} is due to the vibration of Ca and O(1) atoms. Here Ca and O(1) atom performs bending bond vibration. The evaluated frequency at 368 cm^{-1} is due to the vibration of O(2) and O(3) atoms.

The evaluated phonon frequency at 411 cm^{-1} is due to the vibration of Ca and O(1) atoms and Ca atom is 180° out of phase to O(1) atoms which performs bending bond vibration. The evaluated infra-red phonon frequency at 449 cm^{-1} is due to the vibration of O(3), Cu(1) and O(2) atoms and O(2) atoms is 180° out of phase to O(3) and Cu(1) atoms. The highest evaluated infra-red phonon frequency 574 cm^{-1} in E_u symmetry is due to the vibration of O(1) atom which is performing stretching vibration.

Vibrational modes on the region 400-500 cm^{-1} are attributed to Ca-O stretching. The present potential energy distribution confirms our conclusion. The lower frequency modes involve the small displacement of Ca-O and Ba-O and the angular displacement of O-Ca-O. The evaluated frequencies using the normal coordinate analysis method listed in Table 4.16.

REFERENCES

1. Inorganic Infra-red and Ramnd Spectra by S.D. Rose, McGraw-Hill Book Company, England, 1972.
2. Elements of Spectroscopy by S.L. Gupta, V. Kumar, R.C. Sharma, Pragati Prakashan, India, 1983.
3. Infra-red Spectroscopy by R.T. Conley Allyn & Bacon Ltd., 1966.
4. Molecular Spectra and Molecular Structure : Vol. 2, Infra-red and Raman Spectra of Poly Atomic Molecules, G. Herzberg, Van Nostrand, USA, 1945.
5. Infra-red Spectra of Inorganic and Co-ordination Compounds, K. Nakamotao. John Wiley, New York, 1st Edition 1963.
6. Fundametnals of Molecular Spectroscopy by C.N. Banwell, Tata McGraw-Hill Book Company, New Delhi, Second Edition 1975.
7. Introduction to Infra-red and Raman Spectroscopy, S.E. Wiberley, N.B Colthup and L.H. Daly Academic Press (New York), 1st Edition 1964.
8. Theory of Molecular Spectra, W.A. Bingal, Wiley, 1969.
9. Chemical Applications of Group Theory, F. Albert Cotton, Wiley Eastern Ltd., Second Edition 1971.
10. Vibration Spectra and Structure of Polyatomic Molecules, T.Y.Wu, National University of Peking, Kun-ming China, 1939.
11. J.C. Decius, J.Chem. Phy. 22, 1941 (1954).
12. Molecular Vibration by E.Bright Wilson Jr., J.C. Decius and P.C. Cross, McGraw-Hill Book Company, New York, First Edition (1955).
13. E.B.Wilson, J.Chem. Phys. 7, 1047 (1939).
14. Group Theory Applications to Molecular Vibrations by P.G. Puranik, S. Chand & Company Ltd., First Edition (1979).

15. Y. Marino and K. Kuchitsu, J Che. Phy. 20 1809 (1952).
16. E. Bright Wilson, J.Chem. Phy. 9 76 (1941).
17. Molecular Symmetry, D. Schonland, D Van Nostrand, London, McGRaw-Hill Book Company, 1st Edition (1965).
18. S.Mohan and A.Sudha, Pramana J. Phys. 37, 4, 327, (1991).
19. C.Thomsen, M.Cardona, W.Kress, R.Liu. L. Genzel, M Bauer, E. Schonherr and U Schroder, Solid State Commun. 65 (1983) 1139.
20. H. Fuhrer, V.B. Kartha, K.G.Kidd, P.J. Krueger, and H.H. Mantasch, Computer Programmes for Infra-red Spectrometry, Vol. V, Normal Coordinate Analysis National Research Council of Canada, Ottawa 1976.

CHAPTER

5

Comparative Study of Lattice Dynamics and High Temperature Super Conductors

Introduction

This chapter deals with the comparative study between Lattice dynamics and normal coordinate analysis of high temperature superconductors $GdBa_2Cu_3O_7$, $SmBa_2Cu_3O_7$, $EuBa_2Cu_3O_6$, $Tl_2Ca_3Ba_2Cu_4O_{12}$, $Tl_2Ba_2Cu_1O_6$, $TlCa_3Ba_2Cu_4O_{11}$, $Tl_2Ca_2Ba_2Cu_3O_{10}$ and $TlCaBa_2Cu_2O_7$. In the present investigation the lattice dynamical calculations and normal coordinate analysis yield same phonon frequency a bridge between Solid State Physics and Spectroscopy to understand the mechanism of superconductivity. Raman and infra-red studies of these HTSC have contributed significantly to their understanding. The assignment of the spectral features to specific lattice vibrations would be an important step in understanding their role in superconductivity.

The lattice dynamics method is suited to determine the phonon frequencies in the proximity of the Brillouin zone centre only. But, the force constants obtained from that analysis do not provide a stable dynamics throughout the Brillouin zone. However, it is indispensable to have a precise knowledge of the zone–boundary phonons to investigate the contribution of electron-phonon coupling to T_c which can be achieved by neutron scattering techniques. The most commonly employed model is the valence force field model for computing phonon frequencies based on stretching bond and bending bond coordinates. Such models have the advantage of being well adopted to describe a covalent bonding but ignored the long-range Coulomb forces and wave vector dependence of the phonon spectrum. This work considered only the $q = o$ modes and the number of model parameters exceeded the number of experimental data. The rigid ion model on the other hand, considers both the short-range repulsive interactions and the long range Coulomb interaction among various rigid ions in the crystal. The lattice dynamics of high temperature of high temperature superconductor have been performed using rigid ion model. The modified three body shell model adopted in the lattice dynamical study gives favourable phonon frequencies.

Comparative Study of $GdBa_2Cu_3O_7$

The lattice dynamical calculation based on modified TSM reproduce the observed frequencies of Raman and infra-red active modes reasonably which are given in Table 5.1 along with calculated normal coordinate analysis frequencies and the observed frequencies.

Table 5.1. Calculated Phonon frequencies of $GdBa_2Cu_3O_7$ (Values in the Parentheses are experiment frequencies).

Symmetry Species	Frequency (cm^{-1}) Using Lattice Dynamics	Using Normal Coordinate analysis	Potential Energy Distribution (%)
1	2	3	4
A_{1g} (Raman)	555 (550)	560	f_b (70)f_e(10)
	436 (435)	435	f_l (50)f_k(20)
	420 (425)	421	f_k (50)f_n(21)

1	2	3	4
	325 (320)	322	f_p (60) f_a(18)f_e(15)
	165 (162)	160	f_g (64)f_i(20)
B_{2g}	570 (580)	560	f_c (52) f_{im}(60) f_β (18)
	545 (550)	530	f_c (70)
	470 (480)	450	f_h (80)
	310 (320)	310	f_β (70)f_g(25)
	150 (145)	150	f_g (60)f_n(20)
B_{3g}	638 (640)	640	f_c (59)f_α(20)
	578 (580)	580	f_c (84)
	572 (565)	572	f_h (90)
	290 (270)	290	f_β (50)f_i(19)
	114 (110)	115	f_g (54)f_m(30) $f_{i(}$ (15)
B_{1u}	648 (650)	645	f_b (50)f_β(20) f_m (20)
	500 (510)	543	f_b (71) f_β (71)
	485 (480)	482	f_k (50)f_α(11)
	415 (420)	415	f_n (51) f_k (20) f_m(15)
	275 (270)	270	f_c (64)f_b(20)
	180 (180)	180	f_l (30)f_k(20)
	122 (120)	120	f_α (64)f_β(32)f_g(10)
B_{2u}	635 (630)	638	f_β (48)f_c(30) f_m(20)
	628 (620)	625	f_a (78) f_g (15)
	580 (575)	580	f_α (85)
	572 (560)	570	f_h (42) f_e(20) f_α (12)
	212 (212)	200	f_α (68)f_h(30)
	195 (180)	180	f_m (70) f_β (20)
	118 (118)	118	f_k (68) f_α (15)
B_{3u}	640 (635)	640	f_α (41)f_n(28)f_c(20)
	576 (580)	575	f_c(70)f_m(20)
	535 (540)	530	f_h (78)
	450 (420)	455	f_g (78)f_r(21)
	190 (180)	190	f_γ(82)
	180 (175)	180	f_n (48) f_β(30)

The calculated Raman phonon frequency in lattice dynamics at 165 cm^{-1} in A_{1g} symmetry is due to the vibration of Gd atom which agrees very well with the normal coordinate analysis's frequency at 160 cm^{-1} and it is due to the bending vibration of O(2)–Gd -O(3) which is confirmed by the potential energy distribution calculation. The highest frequency in this symmetry in lattice dynamical is 555 cm^{-1}, which is equal to 560 cm^{-1} in normal coordinate analysis which is due to the vibration of O(2) and this phonon frequency is due to the stretched vibration of O(2).

The phonon frequency in lattice dynamics in B_{2g} at 150 cm^{-1} in lattice dynamics is equal to the phonon frequency 150 cm^{-1} obtained by the normal coordinate analysis. This phonon frequency is due to the bending vibration. Similarly, the phonon frequency 310 cm^{-1} and 470 cm^{-1} in lattice dynamical calculation agrees very well with the frequencies obtained by the normal coordinate analysis at 310 cm^{-1} and 450 cm^{-1} respectively. Both these frequency are obtained in the bending vibration mode.

The phonon frequency in lattice dynamics in B_{3g} at 114 cm^{-1} in lattice dynamics is equal to the phonon frequency 115 cm^{-1} obtained by the normal coordinate analysis. This phonon frequency is due to the bending vibration. Similarly, the phonon frequency 290 cm^{-1} and 572 cm^{-1} in lattice dynamical calculation agrees very well with the frequencies obtained by the normal coordinate analysis at 290 cm^{-1} and 572 cm^{-1} respectively. Both these frequency are obtained in the bending vibration mode.

The minimum infra-red phonon frequency in B_{1u} at 122 cm^{-1} in lattice dynamical calculation is due to the vibration of Gd atom which agrees very well with the frequency obtained by the normal coordinate analysis at 120 cm^{-1} which is performed by stretching vibration and it is confirmed by the potential energy distribution calculation. The maximum frequency in this symmetry is 648 cm^{-1} in lattice dynamics which agrees very well with the frequency obtained by the normal coordinate analysis at 645 cm^{-1} is due to the stretched vibration of O(3), which is confirmed by PED calculation.

The phonon frequency in lattice dynamics at 628cm^{-1}in B_{2u} symmetry is due to the vibration of Gd atom agrees very well with the frequency obtained by the normal coordinate analysis at 621 cm^{-1} which is due to bending vibration. Finally, the phonon frequency in this symmetry at 635 cm^{-1} in lattice dynamics agrees with the frequencies obtained by normal coordinate analysis at 638 cm^{-1} is due to the stretched vibration of O(3) atoms which is confirmed by the PED calculation.

The phonon frequency in lattice dynamics at 118 cm^{-1} in E_u symmetry is due to the vibration of Gd atom agrees very well with the frequency obtained by the normal coordinate analysis at 118 cm^{-1} which is due to bending vibration. Finally, the phonon frequency in this symmetry at 580 cm^{-1} in lattice dynamics agrees with the frequencies obtained by normal coordinate analysis at 580 cm^{-1} is due to the stretched vibration of O(3) atoms which is confirmed by the PED calculation.

The phonon frequency in lattice dynamics at 180 cm^{-1} at B_{3u} mode is due to the vibration of Gd atoms agrees very well with the frequency obtained by the normal coordinate analysis at 180 cm^{-1} which is due to bending vibration. The phonon frequency in this symmetry at 190 cm^{-1} in lattice dynamics agrees with the frequencies obtained by normal coordinate analysis at 190 cm^{-1} is due to the bending vibration of Ba atoms. The phonon frequencies in lattice dynamics in B_{3u} mode at 450 cm^{-1}, 535 cm^{-1}, 576 cm^{-1} is due to the vibration of Cu,O(1)and O(2) atoms agrees very well with the frequency obtained by the normal coordinate analysis at 455 cm^{-1}, 535 cm^{-1} and 575 cm^{-1} which is due to bending vibration. Finally, the phonon frequency in this symmetry at 640 cm^{-1} in lattice dynamics agrees with the frequencies obtained by normal coordinate analysis at 640 cm^{-1} is due to the stretched vibration of O(3) atoms which is confirmed by the PED calculation.

Comparative Study of $SmBa_2Cu_3O_7$

The observed frequency, calculated frequency by two different methods and Potential Energy Distribution are given in table 5.2.

Table 5.2. Calculated Phonon frequencies of $SmBa_2Cu_3O_7$ (Values in the Parentheses are experiment frequencies)

Symmetry Species	Frequency (cm^{-1}) Using Lattice Dynamics	Using Normal Coordinate analysis	Potential Energy Distribution (%)
1	2	3	4
A_{1g}	555 (550)	560	f_b (70)f_e(10)
	440 (445)	457	f_i (50)f_k(20)
	420 (420)	436	f_k (50)f_n(21)
	220 (215)	328	f_p (60) f_a(18)f_e(15)
	140 (115)	202	f_g (64)f_i(20)
B_{2g}	637 (630)	594	f_c (52) f_{im}(60) f_β (18)
	587 (584)	482	f_c (70)
	482 (480)	450	f_h (80)
	140 (150)	235	f_β (70)f_g(25)
	90 (80)	155	f_g (60)f_n(20)
B_{3g}	640 (625)	600	f_c (59)f_α(20)
	580 (570)	485	f_c (84)
	560 (560)	464	f_h (90)
	125 (127)	230	f_β (50)f_i(19)
	77 (78)	135	f_g (54)f_m(30) f_i (15)
B_{1u}	630 (630)	560	f_b (50)f_β(20) f_m (20)
	580 (575)	490	f_b (71) f_β (71)
	475 (480)	470	f_k (50)f_α(11)

1	2	3	4
	420 (419)	435	f_n (51) f_k (20) f_m(15)
	255 (250)	325	f_c (64)f_b(20)
	190 (180)	250	f_i (30)f_k(20)
	88 (80)	248	f_α (64)f_β(32)f_g(10)
B_{2u}	635 (630)	597	f_β (48)f_c(30) f_m(20)
	612 (610)	590	f_a (78) f_g (15)
	585 (587)	530	f_α (85)
	555 (556)	478	f_h (42) f_e(20) f_α (12)
	190 (180)	280	f_α (68)f_h(30)
	172 (180)	220	f_m (70) f_β (20)
	87 (86)	150	f_k (68) f_α (15)
B_{3u}	650 (665)	580	f_β (41)f_n(28)f_c(20)
	584 (570)	511	f_c(70)f_m(20)
	523 (520)	460	f_h (78)
	463 (465)	400	f_g (78)f_r(21)
	193 (196)	280	f_γ (82)
	150 (145)	233	f_n (48) f_β(30)

The calculated Raman phonon frequency in A_{1g} symmetry at 140 cm^{-1} in lattice dynamics is due to the vibration of Sm atom agrees very well with the phonon frequency at 202 cm^{-1} in normal coordinate analysis, which is due to the stretched vibration. The phonon frequency at 220 cm^{-1} in A_{1g} in lattice dynamics symmetry is due to the vibration of Ba atom which agrees very well with frequency at 328 cm^{-1} in normal coordinate analysis. This vibration is due to the bending bond vibration and is confirmed by PED calculation. The phonon frequency A_{1g} symmetry at 555 cm^{-1} in lattice dynamics agrees very well, with the frequencies at 560 cm^{-1} in normal coordinate analysis is performed by bending vibration is confirmed by the PED calculation

The calculated phonon frequency in B_{2g} symmetry at 90 cm^{-1} is due to the vibration of Sm atom agrees very well with the frequencies at 155 cm^{-1} in normal coordinate analysis is due to the stretching vibration and is confirmed by the observed value.The phonon frequency in B_{2g} symmetry at 637 cm^{-1} in lattice dynamics is due to the vibration of O(2) atom agrees very well with the frequency at 594 cm^{-1} in normal coordinate analysis. The phonon frequency in B_{3g} symmetry at 640 cm^{-1} in lattice dynamics is due to the vibration of O(3) atom agrees very well with the frequency at 600 cm^{-1} in normal coordinate analysis which is due to the stretched Vibration of (3) atom.

The infrared phonon frequencies in B_{1u} symmetry at 420 cm^{-1} in lattice dynamics is due to the vibration Cu atom agrees very well with frequencies at 435 cm^{-1} in normal coordinate analysis, which is due to the bending vibration. The maximum frequency at 630 cm^{-1} in lattice dynamics is due to the vibration of O(3) atom in B_{1u} symmetry which agrees very well with the frequencies at 560 cm^{-1} in normal coordinate analysis.

The infrared phonon frequencies in B_{2u} at 612 cm^{-1} in lattice dynamics agrees very well with the frequency at 590 cm^{-1} in normal coordinate analysis is due to the stretched vibration of O(2) atoms. The infra-red phonon frequency in lattice dynamics at 190 cm^{-1} in E_u symmetry is due to the vibration of Cu atom is due to the bending vibration of O(2)–Sm-O(1) and it agrees with the frequency at 280 cm^{-1} in normal coordinate analysis.

The infrared phonon frequency in lattice dynamics at 585 cm^{-1} in E_u symmetry is due to the vibration of Cu atom is due to the bending vibration of O(3) and it agrees with the frequency at 530 cm^{-1} in normal coordinate analysis.

The infrared phonon frequency in B_{3u} mode at 463 cm^{-1} in lattice dynamics agrees very well with the frequency at 400 cm^{-1} in normal coordinate analysis. Calculation. The phonon frequencies in lattice dynamics in B_{3u} mode at 463 cm^{-1}, 523 cm^{-1}, 584 cm^{-1} is due to the vibration of Cu,O(1)and O(2) atoms agrees very well with the frequency obtained by the normal coordinate analysis at 400 cm^{-1}, 460 cm^{-1} and 511 cm^{-1} which is due to bending vibration. Finally highest the infrared phonon frequency in B_{3u} mode is 650 cm^{-1} in lattice dynamics agrees very well with the frequency at 580 cm^{-1} in normal coordinate analysis is confirmed by Potential Energy Distribution calculation.

Comparative Study of $EuBa_2Cu_3O_6$

The lattice dynamical calculation based on modified TSM reproduce the observed frequencies of Raman and infra-red active modes reasonably which are given in table 5.3 along with calculated normal coordinate analysis frequencies and the observed frequencies.

The calculated Raman phonon frequency at 118 cm^{-1} in A_{1g} symmetry is due to the vibration of Eu atom which agrees very well with the normal coordinate analysis's frequency at 120 cm^{-1} and it is due to the bending vibration of O(2)–Cu-O(3) which is confirmed by the potential energy distribution calculation. The highest frequency in this symmetry in lattice dynamical is 462 cm^{-1}, which is equal to 463 cm^{-1} in normal coordinate analysis which is due to the vibration of O(2) and this phonon frequency is due to the stretched vibration of O(2).

The phonon frequency at 363 cm^{-1} in lattice dynamics is more or less equal to the phonon frequency obtained by the normal coordinate analysis. This phonon frequency is due to the bending vibration.

The phonon frequency 416 cm^{-1} and 4371 cm^{-1} E_g symmetry in lattice dynamical calculation agrees very well with the frequencies obtained by the normal coordinate analysis at 416 cm^{-1} and 437 cm^{-1} respectively. Both these frequency are obtained in the bending vibration mode.

Table 5.3. Calculated Phonon frequencies of $EuBa_2Cu_3O_6$ (Values in theParentheses are experiment frequencies)

Symmetry Species	Frequency (cm^{-1}) Using Lattice Dynamics	Using Normal Coordinate analysis	Potential Energy Distribution (%)
A_{1g} (Raman)	118 (120)	120	f_b (60)f_d(20)f_k(10)
	184 (185)	185	f_i (70)f_d(11)f_p(10)
	431 (435)	437	f_e (55)f_a(31)
	462 (463)	463	f_a (58)fe(30)f_m(11)
$B1_g$	363	362	F_l (68)fd(14)f_m(10)
E_g	80 (85)	86	f_c (61)f_e(11)f_b(15)
	160 (165)	164	f_m (70) f_i(21)
	416 (416)	420	f_a (45)f_g(31)f_n(20)
	437 (437)	437	f_n (64)f_h(21)f_m(15)
	515 (513)	516	F_k(66)fl(20)f_m(15)
A_{2u} (IR)	136 (138)	136	f_n (70)f_a(12)
	162 (163)	169	f_m (65)f_a(19)f_d(15)
	173 (173)	173	f_p (59)f_n(30)
	339 (340)	339	f_p (62)F_b(19)f_n(15)
	497 (496)	498	f_a (60)f_e(21)f_m(16)
B_{2u}	126 (120)	126	f_p (51)f_n(24)f_e(16)
Eu	103 (104)	103	f_b (70)f_e(14)
	134 (133)	132	f_a (65)f_e(22)
	213 (213)	214	f_a (49) f_d (17) f_e(21)
	372 (372)	373	f_a (60)f_b(22)f_k(11)
	415 (411)	418	f_b (66) f_p (21)
	514 (513)	515	f_n (62)f_a(20)

The minimum infra-red phonon frequency in A_{2u} at 136 cm^{-1} in lattice dynamical calculation is due to the vibration of Ba atom which agrees very well with the frequency obtained by the normal coordinate analysis at 138 cm^{-1} which is performed by stretching vibration and it is confirmed by the potential energy distribution calculation. The maximum frequency in this symmetry is 497 cm^{-1} in lattice dynamics which agrees very well with the frequency obtained by the normal coordinate analysis at 4961 cm^{-1} is due to the stretched vibration of O(3), which is confirmed by PED calculation.

The phonon frequency in lattice dynamics at 372 cm^{-1} in E_u symmetry is due to the vibration of O(1) atom agrees very well with the frequency obtained by the normal coordinate analysis at 373 cm^{-1} which is due to bending vibration. Finally, the phonon frequency in this symmetry at 514 cm^{-1} in lattice dynamics agrees with the frequencies obtained by normal coordinate analysis at 513 cm^{-1} is due to the stretched vibration of O(3) atoms which is confirmed by the PED calculation.

Comparative Study of $Tl_2Ca_3Ba_2Cu_4O_{12}$

The observed frequency, calculated frequency by two different methods and Potential Energy Distribution are given in table 5.4.

The calculated Raman phonon frequency in A_{1g} symmetry at 101cm^{-1} in lattice dynamics is due to the vibration of Ba atom agrees very well with the phonon frequency at 107cm^{-1} in normal coordinate analysis, which is due to the stretched vibration. The phonon frequency at 148 cm^{-1} in A_{1g} in lattice dynamics symmetry is due to the vibration of O(2) atom which agrees very well with frequency at 147 cm^{-1} in normal coordinate analysis. This vibration is due to the bending bond vibration and is confirmed by PED calculation. The phonon frequency A_{1g} symmetry at 520 cm^{-1} in lattice dynamics agrees very well, with the frequencies at 530 cm^{-1} in normal coordinate analysis is performed by bending vibration is confirmed by the PED calculation.

Table 5.4. Calculated Phonon frequencies of $Tl_2Ca_3Ba_2Cu_4O_{12}$

Symmetry Species	Frequency (cm^{-1}) Using Lattice Dynamics	Using Normal Coordinate analysis	Potential Energy Distribution (%)
1	2	3	4
A_{1g} (Raman)	101 (104)	107	f_c (58) f_d(24) f_a (11)
	126 (127)	124	f_c (55) f_l (30)
	148 (142)	147	f_l(71) f_d (12) f_p(11)
	256 (256)	256	f_a (51) f_α(20)
	370 (360)	377	f_a (68) f_u(20) f_c (10)
	449 (439)	438	f_a (61) f_c (20) f_m (10)
	528 (528)	530	f_a (59) f_e(29) f_m(11)
	625 (628)	630	F_l (69) f_e(19) f_m(17)
B_{1g}	206	210	f_a (56) f_k (14) f_a (10)
	298	296	f_a(52) f_k (20) f_β (6)
Eg	68 (65)	60	f_c (60) f_e (14) f_β (6)
	107 (107)	110	f_m (70) f_e(18) f_β(10)
	125 (125)	125	f_m (70) f_l (21)
	244 (245)	240	f_e (52) f_m (16) f_c (12)
	3656 (365)	370	f_l(45) f_n(31) f_c(20)
	378 (400)	390	f_a (42) f_g (25) f_n(15)
	399 (410)	405	f_β(56) f_k (17) f_g(16)
	545 (54)	550	f_n (62) f_h (22) f_m(14)
	555 (567)	560	f_α (68) f_n(21)
A2u	79 (79)	80	f_n (70) f_a(24)
	139 (137)	136	f_m(65) f_u(20) f_d(11)
	143 (143)	150	f_m(80) f_l(14)
	160 (167)	165	f_a(81) f_e(16)
	295 (313)	300	f_p(54)f_n(30)

1	2	3	4
	422 (432)	430	$f_p(62)\ f_\beta(18)\ f_n(10)$
	432 (437)	440	$f_a(40)\ f_g(30)\ f_n(10)$
	456 (450)	450	$f_\beta(41)\ f_p(21)\ f_m(26)$
	570 (574)	580	$f_a(60)\ f_e(21)\ f_m(16)$
B2u	126	130	$f_p(54)\ f_n(26)\ f_e(15)$
	284	283	$f_\beta(28)\ f_p(21)$ fu(30) $f_e(19)$
Eu	68 (68)	70	$f_\beta(70)\ f_c(20)$
	107 (107)	110	$f_a(71)\ f_e(20)$
	132 (133)	134	$f_a(46)\ f_d(18)\ f_b(10)$
	247 (247)	247	$f_n(52)\ f_a(17)\ f_e(24)$
	255 (255)	250	$f_a(55)\ f_d(18)\ f_c(10)$
	355 (36)	365	$f_c(61)\ f_e(16)\ f_u(14)$
	375 (372)	378	$f_a(55)\ f_e(14)\ f_u(20)$
	380 (380)	381	$f_p(64)\ f_c(16)$
	455 (455)	460	$f_\beta(66)\ f_p(25)$
	559 (559)	562	$f_n(65)\ f_\alpha(21)$
	568 (568)	570	$f_n(68)\ f_a(25)$

The calculated phonon frequency in E_g symmetry at 125 cm^{-1} is due to the vibration of Cu atom aggress very well with the frequencies at 125 cm^{-1} in normal coordinate analysis is due to the stretching vibration and is confirmed by PED calculation. The phonon frequency in E_g symmetry at 378 cm^{-1} in lattice dynamics is due to the vibration of O(1) atom agrees very well with the frequency at 390 cm^{-1} in normal coordinate analysis. The phonon frequency in E_g symmetry at 555 cm^{-1} in lattice dynamics is due to the vibration of O(4) atom agrees very well with the frequency at 560 cm^{-1} in normal coordinate analysis which is due to the stretched vibration of O(4) atom.

The infra-red phonon frequencies in A_{2u} symmetry at 160 cm^{-1} in lattice dynamics is due to the vibration O(1) atom agrees very well with frequencies at 165 cm^{-1} in normal coordinate analysis, which is due to the bending vibration. The maximum frequency at 570 cm^{-1} in lattice dynamics is due to the vibration of O(3) atom in A_{2u} symmetry which agrees very well with the frequencies at 580 cm^{-1} in normal coordinate analysis.

The infra-red phonon frequencies in E_u at 132 cm^{-1} in lattice dynamics agrees very well with the frequency at 134 cm^{-1} in normal coordinate analysis is due to the stretched vibration of Ca-O(1) atoms. The infra-red phonon frequency in lattice dynamics at 380 cm^{-1} in E_u symmetry is due to the vibration of Ca atom is due to the bending vibration of O(2)–Tl-O(1) and it agrees very well with the frequency at 381 cm^{-1} in normal coordinate analysis.

Finally, the infra-red phonon frequency at 568 cm^{-1} in lattice dynamics agrees very well with the frequency at 570 cm^{-1} in normal coordinate analysis is confirmed by Potential Energy Distribution calculation.

Comparative Study of $Tl_2Ca_3 Ba_2Cu_4O_{11}$

The observed frequency, calculated frequency by two different methods and Potential Energy Distribution are given in table 5.5.

The calculated Raman phonon frequency in A_{1g} symmetry at 101 cm^{-1} in lattice dynamics is due to the vibration of Ba atom agrees very well with the phonon frequency at 107 cm^{-1} in normal coordinate analysis, which is due to the stretched vibration. The phonon frequency at 148 cm^{-1} in A_{1g} in lattice dynamics symmetry is due to the vibration of O(2) atom which agrees very well with frequency at 147 cm^{-1} in normal coordinate analysis. This vibration is due to the bending bond vibration and is confirmed by PED calculation. The phonon frequency A_{1g} symmetry at 520 cm^{-1} in lattice dynamics agrees very well, with the frequencies at 530 cm^{-1} in normal coordinate analysis is performed by bending vibration is confirmed by the PED calculation.

Table 5.5. Calculated Phonon frequencies of $Tl_2Ca_3Ba_2Cu_4O_{11}$

Symmetry Species	Frequency (cm^{-1}) Using Lattice Dynamics	Using Normal Coordinate analysis (Cm^{-1})	Potential Energy Distribution (%)
1	2	3	4
A_{1g} (Raman)	101 (104)	107	f_c(58) f_d(24) f_a(11)
	126 (127)	124	f_c (55) f_l (30)
	148 (142)	147	f_l(71) f_d (12) f_p(11)
	256 (256)	256	f_a (51) $f_{á}$(20)
	370 (360)	377	f_a (68) f_u(20) f_c (10)
	449 (439)	438	f_a (61) f_c (20) f_m (10)
	528 (528)	530	f_a (59) f_e(29) f_m(11)
B_{1g}	206	210	f_a (56) f_k (14) f_a (10)
	298	296	f_a(52) f_k (20) $f_{â}$ (6)
Eg	68 (65)	60	f_c (60) f_e (14) $f_{â}$ (6)
	107 (107)	110	f_m (70) f_e(18) $f_{â}$(10)
	125 (125)	125	f_m (70) f_l (21)
	244 (245)	240	f_e (52) f_m (16) f_c (12)
	3656 (365)	370	f_l(45) f_n(31) f_c(20)
	378 (400)	390	f_a (42) f_g (25) f_n(15)
	399 (410)	405	$f_{â}$(56) f_k (17) f_g(16)
	545 (54)	550	f_n (62) f_h (22) f_m(14)
	555 (567)	560	$f_{á}$ (68) f_n(21)

1	2	3	4
A_{2u}	79 (79)	80	f_n (70) f_a(24)
	139 (137)	136	f_m(65) f_u(20) f_d(11)
	143 (143)	150	f_m (80) f_l(14)
	160 (167)	165	f_a(81) f_e(16)
	295 (313)	300	f_p(54)f_n(30)
	422 (432)	430	f_p(62) $f_{\hat{a}}$(18) f_n(10)
	432 (437)	440	f_a(40) f_g(30) f_n(10)
	456 (450)	450	$f_{\hat{a}}$(41) f_p(21) f_m(26)
	570 (574)	580	f_a(60) f_e(21) f_m(16)
B_{2u}	126	130	f_p(54) f_n(26) f_e(15)
	284	283	$f_{\hat{a}}$(28) f_p(21) fu(30) f_e(19)
E_u	68 (68)	70	$f_{\hat{a}}$(70) f_c(20)
	107 (107)	110	f_a(71) f_e(20)
	132 (133)	134	f_a(46) f_d(18) f_b(10)
	247 (247)	247	f_n(52) f_a(17) f_e(24)
	255 (255)	250	f_a(55) f_d(18) f_c(10)
	355 (36)	365	f_c(61) f_e(16) f_u(14)
	375 (372)	378	f_a(55) f_e(14) f_u(20)
	380 (380)	381	f_p(64) f_c(16)
	455 (455)	460	$f_{\hat{a}}$(66) f_p(25)
	559 (559)	562	f_n(65) $f_{\acute{a}}$(21)
	568 (568)	570	f_n(68) f_a(25)

The calculated phonon frequency in E_g symmetry at 125 cm^{-1} is due to the vibration of Cu atom aggress very well with the frequencies at 125 cm^{-1} in normal coordinate analysis is due to the stretching vibration and is confirmed by

PED calculation. The phonon frequency in E_g symmetry at 378 cm^{-1} in lattice dynamics is due to the vibration of O(1) atom agrees very well with the frequency at 390 cm^{-1} in normal coordinate analysis. The phonon frequency in E_g symmetry at 555 cm^{-1} in lattice dynamics is due to the vibration of O(4) atom agrees very well with the frequency at 560 cm^{-1} in normal coordinate analysis which is due to the stretched vibration of O(4) atom.

The infra-red phonon frequencies in A_{2u} symmetry at 160 cm^{-1} in lattice dynamics is due to the vibration O(1) atom agrees very well with frequencies at 165 cm^{-1} in normal coordinate analysis, which is due to the bending vibration. The maximum frequency at 570 cm^{-1} in lattice dynamics is due to the vibration of O(3) atom in A_{2u} symmetry which agrees very well with the frequencies at 580 cm^{-1} in normal coordinate analysis.

The infra-red phonon frequencies in E_u at 132 cm^{-1} in lattice dynamics agrees very well with the frequency at 134 cm^{-1} in normal coordinate analysis is due to the stretched vibration of Ca-O(1) atoms. The infrared phonon frequency in lattice dynamics at 380 cm^{-1} in E_u symmetry is due to the vibration of Ca atom is due to the bending vibration of O(2)–Tl-O(1) and it agrees very well with the frequency at 381 cm^{-1} in normal coordinate analysis.

Finally, the infra-red phonon frequency at 568 cm^{-1} in lattice dynamics agrees very well with the frequency at 570 cm^{-1} in normal coordinate analysis is confirmed by Potential Energy Distribution calculation.

Comparative Study of $Tl_2Ba_2Cu_1O_6$

The lattice dynamical calculation based on modified TSM and the phonon frequencies obtained by Normal Cordinate Analysis method is reproduced reasonably which are given in table 5.6 (*See on next page*), along with calculated normal coordinate analysis frequencies and the observed frequencies.

The calculated Raman phonon frequency at 124 cm^{-1} in A_{1g} symmetry is due to the vibration of Ba atom which agrees very well with the normal coordinate analysis's frequency at 121 cm^{-1} and it is due to the bending vibration of O(2)–Tl-O(3) which is confirmed by the potential energy distribution calculation. The highest frequency in this symmetry in lattice dynamical is 601 cm^{-1}, which is equal to 602 cm^{-1} in normal coordinate analysis which is due to the vibration of O(2) and this phonon frequency is due to the stretched vibration of O(2).

The phonon frequency at 100 cm^{-1} in lattice dynamics is more or less equal to the phonon frequency obtained by the normal coordinate analysis. This phonon frequency is due to the bending vibration. Similarly, the phonon frequency 308 cm^{-1} and 491 cm^{-1} in lattice dynamical calculation agrees very well with the frequencies obtained by the normal coordinate analysis at 400 cm^{-1} and 499 cm^{-1} respectively. Both these frequency are obtained in the bending vibration mode.

The minimum infrared phonon frequency in A_{2u} at 108 cm^{-1} in lattice dynamical calculation is due to the vibration of Ba atom which agrees very well with the frequency obtained by the normal coordinate analysis at 115 cm^{-1} which is performed by stretching vibration and it is confirmed by the potential energy distribution calculation. The maximum frequency in this symmetry is 656 cm^{-1} in lattice dynamics which agrees very well with the frequency obtained by the normal coordinate analysis at 641 cm^{-1} is due to the stretched vibration of O(3), which is confirmed by PED calculation.

The phonon frequency in lattice dynamics at 320 cm^{-1} in E_u symmetry is due to the vibration of O(1) atom agrees very well with the frequency obtained by the normal coordinate analysis at 321 cm^{-1} which is due to bending vibration. Finally, the phonon frequency in this symmetry at 559 cm^{-1} in lattice dynamics agrees with the frequencies obtained by normal coordinate analysis at 561 cm^{-1} is due to the stretched vibration of O(3) atoms which is confirmed by the PED calculation.

Table 5.6. Calculated Phonon frequencies of $Tl_2Ba_2Cu_1O_6$ (Values in the Parentheses are experiment frequencies)

Symmetry Species	Frequency (cm^{-1}) Using Lattice Dynamics	Using Normal Coordinate analysis	Potential Energy Distribution (%)
A_{1g} (Raman)	124 (125)	121	fb (60)fd(20)fk(10)
	153 (165)	161	fi (70)fd(11)fp(10)
	470 (485)	482	fe (55)fa(31)
	601 (603)	602	fa (58)fe(30)fm(11)
Eg	100	106	fc (61)fe(11)fB(15)
	131	134	fm (70) fi(21)
	388	400	fa (45)fg(31)fn(20)
	491	499	fn (64)fh(21)fm(15)
A_{2u} (IR)	108 (108)	115	fn (70)fa(12)
	141 (143)	139	fm (65)fa(19)fd(15)
	335 (341)	351	fp (59)fn(30)
	443 (451)	441	fp (62)Fb(19)fn(15)
	656 (648)	641	fa (60)fe(21)fm(16)
B_{2u}	259	270	fp (51)fn(24)fe(16)
E_u	84	89	fb (70)fe(14)
	162 (163)	168	fa (65)fe(22)
	320 (326)	321	fa (49) fd (17) fe(21)
	411 (419)	406	fa (60)fb(22)fk(11)
	445 (451)	448	Fb (66) fp (21)
	559 (563)	561	fn (62)fa(20)

Comparative Study of $Tl_2Ca_2Ba_2Cu_3O_{10}$

The phonon frequencies obtained by the Lattice Dynamical Calculations based on modified TSM and by the Normal Coordinate Analysis method reproduces the observed frequencies of Raman and infra-red active modes reasonable which are given in table 5.7 (*See on next page*). The calculated frequencies are in good agreement with the available experimental values. The lowest calculated active A_{1g} mode frequency at 104 cm^{-1} by Lattice dynamics method is due to the vibration of Ba, Cu(1) and Cu(2) atoms and this agrees very well with the observed frequency at 99 cm^{-1} which corresponds to the frequency at 110 cm^{-1} by the method of Normal coordinate analysis method. The evaluated Raman phonon frequency by Lattice dynamics at 126 cm^{-1} is due to the vibration of Tl, Ba and Cu(1) atoms which agrees very well with the normal coordinate analysis's frequency at 130 cm^{-1} and the observed frequency at 133 cm^{-1} agrees very well with the calculated frequency. Here the Tl atom is vibrating 180° out of phase to Ba and Cu(1) atoms. Similarly the Lattice dynamics calculated Raman phonon frequency at 144 cm^{-1} is due to the vibration of Cu(1), Ba and Cu(2) atoms and Ba atom is vibrating 180° out of phase of Cu(1) and Cu(2) atoms which agrees very well with the normal coordinate analysis's frequency at 151 cm^{-1} and the observed frequency at 159 cm^{-1} agrees very well with the calculated frequency. The next calculated Raman phonon frequency lattice dynamics at 290 cm^{-1} is due to the vibration of O(1), O(4) and Ca atoms which agrees very well with the normal coordinate analysis's frequency at 281 cm^{-1} and its observed frequency is 270 cm^{-1}. The evaluated Raman phonon frequency by Lattcice dynamics at 401 cm^{-1} is due to the vibration of O(1), O(4) and Ca atoms and the Ca atom is vibrating 180° out of phase to O (1) and O(4) atoms which agrees very well with the normal coordinate analysis's frequency at 412 cm^{-1} and the observed frequency 407 cm^{-1} agrees very well with the calculated frequency. The evaluated phonon frequency 489 cm^{-1} is due to Vibration of O(2) atoms. The maximum evaluated Raman frequency by

Table 5.7. Calculated Phonon frequencies of $Tl_2Ca_2Ba_2Cu_3O_{10}$ (Values in the Parentheses are experimental frequencies)

Symmetry Species	Frequency (cm^{-1}) Using Lattice Dynamics	Using Normal Coordinate analysis	Potential Energy Distribution (%)
1	2	3	4
A_{1g}(Raman)	104 (99)	110	$f_{\hat{a}}(60)f_d(19)f_k(14)$
	126 (133)	130	$f_c(55)f_l(30)$
	144 (159)	151	$f_e(72)f_l(19)$
	290 (270)	281	$f_a(51)f_{\acute{a}}(29)$
	401 (407)	412	$f_a(61)f_c(20)f_m(10)$
	489 (498)	486	$f_a(52)f_k(21)f_c(13)$
	608 (601)	605	$f_a(72)f_{\acute{a}}(16)$
B_{1g}	256 (245)	261	$f_a(56)f_k(14)f_{\acute{a}}(10)$
E_g	66	70	$f_c(60)f_e(14)f_{\hat{a}}(16)$
	136	142	$f_m(74)f_e(20)$
	140	164	$f_e(41)f_m(20)f_l(19)$
	259	270	$f_e(52)f_m(16)f_c(12)$
	375	365	$f_a(42)f_g(33)f_n(16)$
	415	411	$f_{\hat{a}}(51)f_k(12)f_g(19)$
	489	471	$f_n(65)f_h(20)f_m(17)$
	555	554	$f_{\acute{a}}(61)f_m(21)$
A_{2u}(IR)	72 (103)	81	$f_n(70)f_{\acute{a}}(24)$
	128 (131)	120	$f_m(68)f_k(24)f_{\acute{a}}(12)$
	150 (151)	148	$f_a(80)f_e(14)$
	190 (197)	181	$f_a(74)f_e(20)$
	365 (372)	369	$f_p(54)f_n(30)$
	420 (421)	411	$f_p(62)f_{\hat{a}}(18)f_n(10)$

1	2	3	4
	444 (454)	449	$f_p(66)f_{â}(20)f_{ç}(10)$
	607 (616)	592	$f_{â}(40)f_{â}(19)f_n(11)$
B_{2u}	133	138	$f_p(54)f_n(26)f_e(15)$
	306	309	$f_a(40)f_g(35)f_n(10)$
E_u	70 (70)	69	$f_{â}(70)f_c(20)$
	101 (101)	105	$f_a(66)f_e(21)$
	145 (145)	152	$f_a(71)f_c(20)$
	225 (225)	228	$f_a(41)f_{á}(14)f_c(21)$
	359 (359)	358	$f_c(61)f_e(16)f_k(14)$
	387 (397)	390	$f_{â}(64), f_c$
	435 (446)	441	$f_{â}(56), f_g$
	451 (456)	458	$f_{â}(64)f_p(28)$
	555 (556)	562	$f_n(65)f_{á}(21)$
	569 (563)	571	$f_{ç}(71)f_{á}(20)$

Lattice dynamics at 608 cm^{-1} is due to the vibration of O(3) atoms which agrees very well with the normal coordinate analysis's frequency at 605 cm^{-1} and the observed frequency 601 cm^{-1} agrees very well with the calculated frequency. The evaluated Raman phonon frequency by Lattice dynamics at 256 cm^{-1} in B_{1g} Symmetry is due to the vibration of O(1) and O (4) atoms which agrees very well with the normal coordinate analysis's frequency at 261 cm^{-1} and the observed frequency 245 cm^{-1} agrees very well with calculated frequency is confirmed by Potential Energy Distribution calculation.

Similarly, the evaluated Raman phonon frequency by Lattice dynamics at 66 cm^{-1} in Eg symmetry is due to the vibration of Ba, Cu(1) atoms which agrees very well with the normal coordinate analysis's frequency at 70 cm^{-1} and are in plane with Ca atom. The Raman phonon frequency by Lattice dynamics at 136 cm^{-1} is due to the vibration of Tl atom which agrees very well with the normal coordinate analysis's frequency at 142 cm^{-1}. The evaluated Raman frequency by Lattice dynamics at 140 cm^{-1} is due to Cu(1), Ba and Ca atoms and Ba atom is vibrating 180 out of phase of Cu(1) and Ca atoms which agrees very well with the normal coordinate analysis's frequency at 164 cm^{-1}. The evaluated phonon frequency by Lattice dynamics at 259 cm^{-1} is due to the bending vibration of O(1), O(4) and Ca atoms which agrees very well with the normal coordinate analysis's frequency at 270 cm^{-1}. The phonon frequency by Lattice dynamics at 375 cm^{-1} due to stretching vibration of O(1) and O(4) atoms which agrees very well with the normal coordinate analysis's frequency at 365 cm^{-1}. The calculated phonon frequency by Lattice dynamics at 415 cm^{-1} is due to the vibration of O(2) atoms which agrees very well with the normal coordinate analysis's frequency at 411 cm^{-1}. The phonon frequency by Lattice dynamics at 489 cm^{-1} is due to the vibration of O(3) atom which agrees very well with the normal coordinate analysis's frequency at 471 cm^{-1}. The highest calculated phonon frequency by Lattice dynamics at 555 cm^{-1} in Eg symmetry is due to the stretching vibration of O(1) atoms which agrees very well with the normal coordinate analysis's frequency at 554 cm^{-1} is confirmed by Potential Energy Distribution calculation.

The lowest calculated infra-red phonon frequency by Lattice dynamics in A_{2u} symmetry at 72 cm^{-1} is due to the vibrations of $C_u(1)$ and $C_u(2)$ atoms which agrees very well with the normal coordinate analysis's frequency at 81 cm^{-1} and the observed frequency at 103 cm^{-1} agrees very well with the calculated frequency. The evaluated infra-red phonon frequency by Lattice dynamics at 128 cm^{-1} is due to the vibration of Cu(2), Cu(1) and Tl atoms in which Tl atom vibrates 180° out of phase to Cu(2) and Cu(1) atoms which agrees very well with the normal coordinate analysis's frequency at 120 cm^{-1} and the observed frequency 131 cm^{-1} agrees very well with the calculated frequency. The next evaluated infra-red phonon frequency by Lattice dynamics at 150 cm^{-1} is due to the vibration of Cu(2) and Cu(1) atoms which agrees very well with the normal coordinate analysis's frequency at 148 cm^{-1} and the observed frequency at 151 cm^{-1} agrees very well with the calculated frequency is confirmed by Potential Energy Distribution calculation.

The evaluated infra-red phonon frequency by Lattice dynamics at 190 cm^{-1} is due to the vibration of O(4), O(1) and Ca atoms which agrees very well with the normal coordinate analysis's frequency at 181 cm^{-1} and its observed frequency 197 cm^{-1} agrees very well with the calculated phonon frequency. The next evaluated infra-red phonon frequency by Lattice dynamics at 365 cm^{-1} is due to the vibration of O(2), Ca and O(1) atoms. Here Ca atom is vibrating 180° out of phase to O(2) and O(1) atoms which agrees very well with the normal coordinate analysis's frequency at 369 cm^{-1} and the observed frequency at 372 cm^{-1} agrees very well with the calculated frequency. The calculated frequency by Lattice dynamics at 420 cm^{-1} is due the vibration of O(4), O(2) and Ca atoms in which Ca atom vibrates 180° out of phase to O(4) and O(2) atoms which agrees very well with the normal coordinate analysis's frequency at 411 cm^{-1} and the observed frequency 421 cm^{-1} agrees very well with the calculated frequency. The next higher calculated infra-red phonon frequency by Lattice dynamics at 444 cm^{-1} is due to the vibration of O(2), O(1) and Ca atoms which agrees very well with the normal coordinate analysis's frequency at 449 cm^{-1} and the observed frequency at 454 cm^{-1} agrees very well with the calculated frequency. The highest calculated infra-red phonon frequency in A_{2u} symmetry by Lattice dynamics at 607 cm^{-1} is due to the vibration of O(3) atom which agrees very well with the normal coordinate analysis's frequency at 592 cm^{-1} and its observed frequency at 616 cm^{-1} agrees very well with the calculated frequency is confirmed by Potential Energy Distribution calculation.

The evaluated phonon infra-red frequency in B_{2u} symmetry by Lattice dynamics at 133 cm^{-1} is due to the vibration of O(4) and O(1) atoms which agrees very well with the normal coordinate analysis's frequency at 138 cm^{-1}. The calculated frequency by Lattice dynamics at 306 cm^{-1} is due to the vibration of O(4) and O(1) atoms which agrees very well with the normal coordinate analysis's frequency at 309 cm^{-1} is confirmed by Potential Energy Distribution calculation.

The lowest calculated infra-red phonon frequency by Lattice dynamics in Eu symmetry is 70 cm^{-1} which is due to the vibration of Cu(2) and Tl atoms and the Tl atom is vibrating out of plane to Cu(2) atom which agrees very well with the normal coordinate analysis's frequency at 69 cm^{-1} and the observed frequency 70 cm^{-1} agrees very well with the calculated frequency. The calculated infra-red frequency by Lattice dynamics at 101 cm^{-1} is due to the vibration of Tl and Cu(2) atoms which agrees very well with the normal coordinate analysis's frequency at 105 cm^{-1} and the observed frequency at 101 cm^{-1} agrees very well with the calculated phonon frequency. The evaluated infra-red phonon frequency by Lattice dynamics at 145 cm^{-1} is due to the vibration of Cu(1), Cu(2) and Ba atoms in which Ba atom is vibrating 180° out of phase to Cu(1) and Cu(2) atoms which agrees very well with the normal coordinate analysis's frequency at 152 cm^{-1} and the observed frequency at 145 cm^{-1} agrees very well with the calculated frequency. The calculated infra-red frequency by Lattice dynamics at 255 cm^{-1} is due to vibration of Cu O(4) and O(1) atoms which performs bending bond vibrations which agrees very well with the normal coordinate analysis's frequency at 228 cm^{-1} and the observed frequency at 255 cm^{-1} agrees very well with the calculated frequency. The next calculated infra-red frequency by Lattice dynamics at 359 cm^{-1} is due to the vibration of O(4) and O(1) atoms which agrees very well with the normal coordinate analysis's frequency at 358 cm^{-1} and the observed frequency at 359 cm^{-1} agrees very well with the calculated frequency. The calculated infra-red phonon frequency Lattice dynamics at 387 cm^{-1} is due to the vibration of O(2) and O(3) atoms which agrees very well with the normal coordinate analysis's frequency at 390 cm^{-1} and the observed frequency at 397

cm^{-1} agrees very well with the calculated frequency is confirmed by Potential Energy Distribution calculation.

The calculated infra-red phonon frequency by Lattice dynamics at 435 cm^{-1} is due to the vibration of Ca, O(1) and O(4) atoms. Here Ca atom vibrates 180° out of phase to O(1) and O(4) atoms which agrees very well with the normal coordinate analysis's frequency at 441 cm^{-1} and the observed frequency at 446 cm^{-1} agrees very well with the calculated frequency. The evaluated frequency by Lattice dynamics at 451 cm^{-1} is due to the vibration of O(3) and O(2) atoms and the O(2) atom vibraties out of plane to O(3) atom which agrees very well with the normal coordinate analysis's frequency at 458 cm^{-1} and the observed frequency at 456 cm^{-1} agrees very well with the calculated frequency. The evaluated infra-red frequency by Lattice dynamics at 555 cm^{-1} is due to the vibration of O(1) atom which performs stretching vibrations which agrees very well with the normal coordinate analysis's frequency at 562 cm^{-1} and the observed frequency at 556 cm^{-1} agrees very well with the calculated frequency. The highest calculated infra-red frequency by Lattice dynamics in Eu symmetry at 569 cm^{-1} is due to the vibration of O(4) atom performs stretching vibration which agrees very well with the normal coordinate analysis's frequency at 571 cm^{-1} and the observed frequency 563cm^{-1} agrees very well with the calculated frequency is confirmed by Potential Energy Distribution calculation.

Comparative Study of $TlCaBa_2Cu_2O_7$

The Phonon frequencies obtained by the lattice dynamical calculations based on a modified TSM reproduce the observed frequencies of Raman and infra-red modes reasonably and the frequencies obtained by the method of Normal Cordinate Analysis method are given in Table 5.8. The calculated frequencies are in good agreement with the available experimental values. The evaluated Raman phonon frequencies by the method lattice dynamics 123, 137, 468,

Table 5.8. Calculated Phonon frequencies of $TlCaBa_2Cu_2O_7$ (Values in the Parentheses are experimental frequencies).

Symmetry Species	Frequency (cm^{-1}) Using Lattice Dynamics	Using Normal Coordinate analysis	Potential Energy Distribution (%)
A_{1g}(Raman)	123 (120)	126	$f_{â}$ (51)f_d(20)f_k(11)
	137 (148)	161	f_c (66) f_l (21)
	468 (485)	462	f_a (71)f_k(11)f_c(11)
	509 (525)	498	f_a (68)$f_{á}$ (34)
B_{1g}	296 (278)	289	f_a (52)f_k(20)$f_{â}$(11)
E_g	80	81	f_c (58)f_e(11)$f_{â}$ (11)
	138	141	f_m (70)f_l(20)
	338	342	f_l(41)f_m(21)f_c(18)
	396	400	f_a (40)f_g(30)f_n(10)
	565	572	$f_{á}$ (71)f_n(19)
A_{2u} (IR)	95 (103)	101	f_n (70)$f_{á}$ (19)
	125 (134)	131	f_m (66)f_c(19)$f_{á}$(11)
	214 (224)	219	f_a(81)f_e(16)
	349 (433)	345	f_p (60)$f_{â}$(17)f_n(11)
	445 (449)	451	$f_{â}$ (72)$f_{â}$(16)f_n(10)
	546 (566)	548	$f_{â}$ (44)f_p(20)f_m(25)
B_{2u}	189	192	f_p (44)f_n(21)f_e(17)
E_u	97 (97)	98	f_p (70)f_c(16)
	124 (124)	131	$f_{á}$ (72)f_c(20)
	240 (240)	241	f_n (52)$f_{á}$ (17)f_e(24)
	371 (375)	368	f_a (55)f_e(14)f_k(20)
	405 (419)	411	$f_{á}$ (64)f_p(14)f_k(15)
	448 (448)	449	$f_{â}$ (66)f_p(25)
	567 (570)	574	f_n (68)$f_{á}$ (25)

509 cm^{-1} in A_{1g} symmetry are due to the vibration of Ba, Cu(1), O(1) and O(2) atoms respectively and its observed frequencies 120, 148, 489 and 525 cm^{-1} agrees very well with the calculated phonon frequencies. The frequenies obtained by the Normal Cordinate Analysis in this symmetry are 126, 161, 462, 498 cm^{-1} agrees very well with the calculated frequencies by lattice dynamics method. Further the evaluated calculated phonon frequency 296 cm^{-1} in B_{1g} symmetry is due to the vibration of O(1) atom and the observed value 278 cm^{-1} agrees very well with the calculated frequency. The frequency at 289 cm^{-1} in this symmetry obtained by the Normal coordinate Analysis method agrees very well with the calculated phonon frequencies by the lattice dynamics method.

The calculated phonon frequencies by lattice dynamics method at 80, 138, 338, 396 and 565 cm^{-1} in Eg symmetry are due to the vibration of Ba, C_u(1), Ca, O(2) and O(1) atoms respectively. The Phonon frequencies obtained by the Normal Coordinate Analysis method are 81, 141, 342, 400 and 572 cm^{-1}. Frequencies obtained by both the methods agrees very well with each other is confirmed by Potential Energy Distribution calculation.

The lowest evaluated infra-red frequency by Lattice dynamics method at 95 cm^{-1} in A_{2u} symmetry is due to the vibration of Cu(1) atom and the observed frequency at 103 cm^{-1} agrees very well with the evaluated frequency. This frequency corresponds to 101 cm^{-1} in Normal Co-ordinate Analysis method. The evaluated infra-red frequency at 125 cm^{-1} is due to the vibration of Tl and Ba atoms. Here also the observed frequency at 134 cm^{-1} agrees very well with the evaluated phonon frequency which corresponds to the frequency at 131 cm^{-1} in Normal Coordinate Analysis method. The evaluated infra-red frequency at 214 cm^{-1} is due to the vibration of Cu and O(1) atoms and its observed frequency 224 cm^{-1} agrees very well with the calculated frequency which cooresponds to the frequency at 219 cm^{-1} in Normal Cordinate

Analysis method. The evaluated infra-red phonon frequency at 349 cm^{-1} is due to the vibration of O(2) and Ca atoms and the observed frequency 433 cm^{-1} agrees very well with the evaluated phonon frequency which corresponding to the frequency at 345 cm^{-1} in Normal coordinate Analysis method. The evaluated phonon frequency at 445 cm^{-1} is due to the vibrations of Ca,O(2) and O(1) atoms in which O(1) atom is 180^0 out of phase to Cu and O(2) atoms and the observed frequency at 449 cm^{-1} agrees very well with the calculated value which corresponds to the frequency at 451 cm^{-1} in Normal coordinate Analysis method. The highest infra-red phonon frequency in A_{2u} symmetry at 546 cm^{-1} due to the vibration of O(3) atoms which agrees very well with the observed frequency at 566 cm^{-1} which coorsponds to the frequency at 548 cm^{-1}. frequencies obtained by both the methods agrees very well with each other. The infra-red phonon frequency at 189 cm^{-1} in B_{2u} symmetry is due to the vibration of O(1) atom which corresponds to the frequency at 192 cm^{-1} is confirmed by Potential Energy Distribution calculation.

The lowest infra-red phonon frquency in E_u symmetry at 97 cm^{-1} is due to the vibration of Tl and Cu(1) atoms and its observed frequency at 97 cm^{-1} agrees very well with the evaluated value. The phonon frequency at 98 cm^{-1} obtained by Normal Coordinate Analysis method agrees well with the calculated phonon frequencies by the Lattice Dynamics method. The next infra-red phonon frequency 124 cm^{-1} by the lattice dynamics method in E_u symmetry is due to the vibration of Ca, Ba and Cu(1) atoms where atom Ba is 180^0 out of phase to Cu and Ca atoms. Here the observed frequency 124 cm^{-1} agrees very well with the evaluated frequency which corresponds to the frequency at 131 cm^{-1} in Normal coordinate Analysis method. The evaluated frequency at 240 cm^{-1} is due to the vibration of Ca and O(1) atoms and the observed frequency 240 cm^{-1} is very close to the calculated frequency.

The frequency at 241 cm^{-1} obtained method of Normal Coordinate Analysis methods agrees very well with each other. Here Ca and O(1) atom performs bending bond vibration. The evaluated frequency at 371 cm^{-1} is due to the vibration of O(2) and O(3) atoms and its observed frequency at 375 cm^{-1} agrees very well with the calculated frequency which cooresponds to the frequency at 368 cm^{-1} in Normal Coordinate Analysis method is confirmed by Potential Energy Distribution calculation.

The evaluated phonon frequency at 405 cm^{-1} by lattice dynamics method is due to the vibration of Ca and O(1) atoms and Ca atom is 180° out of phase to O(1) atoms which performs bending bond vibration and the observed frequency at 419 cm^{-1} agrees very well with the calculated frequency which cooresponds to the frequency at 411 cm^{-1} in Noormal Coordinate Analysis method. The evaluated infra-red phonon frequency at 448 cm^{-1} is due to the vibration of O(3), Cu(1) and O(2) atoms and O(2) atoms is 180° out of phase to O(3) and Cu(1) atoms and the observed frequency at 448 cm^{-1} agrees very well with the observed frequency which cooresponds to the frequency at 449 cm^{-1} in Normal Coordinate Anslysis method. The highest evaluated infra-red phonon frequency 567 cm^{-1} in E_u symmetry is due to the vibration of O(1) atom which is performing stretching vibration and its experimentally observed frequency 570 cm^{-1} agrees very well with the calculated frequency. The Phonon frequency at 574 cm^{-1} obtained by Normal Coordinate Anslysis method agrees well with the phonon frequency by the method of Lattice Dynamics is confirmed by Potential Energy Distribution calculation.

Conclusion

In this work, two different methods viz, lattice dynamical study and normal coordinate analysis yielded the same phonon frequency for high temperature superconductor

$GdBa_2Cu_3O_7$, $SmBa_2Cu_3O_7$, $EuBa_2Cu_3O_6$, $Tl_2Ca_3Ba_2Cu_4O_{12}$, $Tl_2Ba_2Cu_1O_6$, $TlCa_3Ba_2Cu_4O_{11}$, $Tl_2Ca_2Ba_2Cu_3O_{10}$ and $TlCaBa_2Cu_2O_7$. It is also seen from the tables, that the agreement between the calculated and observed frequencies wherever available are very good for the systems under consideration.

Therefore, it is concluded that metal-oxide (Cu-O) plays an important role for the occurrence of superconductivity. The Raman scattering has provided direct evidence for strong electron–phonon interaction in the high T_c superconducting oxides. The vibrational frequencies calculated by the methods of Lattice Dynamics and Normal Coordinate Analysis are compared and they appear to be in good agreement, which is confirmed by the Potential Energy Distribution calculation.

Index

M

N